BIBLE MATRIX

Mike Bull is a graphic designer who lives and works in the Blue Mountains west of Sydney, Australia. His passion is understanding and teaching the Bible.

BIBLE

AN INTRODUCTION TO THE
DNA OF THE SCRIPTURES

MATRIX

Unless otherwise indicated, all Scripture quotations are taken from *The Holy Bible, English Standard Version* copyright 2001 by Crossway Bibles, a publishing ministry of Good New Publishers. Used by permission. All rights reserved.

WestBow Press books may be ordered through booksellers or by contacting:

WestBow Press
A Division of Thomas Nelson
1663 Liberty Drive
Bloomington, IN 47403
www.westbowpress.com
1-(866) 928-1240

Because of the dynamic nature of the Internet, any Web addresses or links contained in this book may have changed since publication and may no longer be valid. The views expressed in this work are solely those of the author and do not necessarily reflect the views of the publisher, and the publisher hereby disclaims any responsibility for them.

ISBN: 978-1-4497-0263-2 (sc)
ISBN: 978-1-4497-0264-9 (hc)
ISBN: 978-1-4497-0262-5 (e)

Library of Congress Control Number: 2010928775

Cover illustration: *The Temptation in Eden* by Michael O'Brien
www.studiobrien.com

Tabernacle images used by permission from www.the-tabernacle-place.com

Printed in the United States of America

WestBow Press rev. date: 1/27/2011

For James B. Jordan
who gave us new eyes

CONTENTS

FOREWORD

PETER J. LEITHART

BEGINNINGS ARE SEEDS. Plants grow up from seeds. So do animals, and humans too. Seeds are beginnings, but seeds also initiate a process of growth that will be fulfilled in the middle and end. So beginnings contain endings. Mighty oaks from tiny acorns grow, but mighty hippos do not. For that, you need some hippo seed and preferably a female incubator to nourish it along. It is certainly one-sided, but T. S. Eliot had something right when he said, in *East Coker*, "In my beginning is my end." As seed, we already are from the beginning what we will become.

Texts are not organisms, but for writers who are in control of their tools and materials, textual beginnings are also seeds that determine what sort of text will spring up. No book illustrates this more clearly than the Bible, which begins in a well-watered garden full of fruit trees and peaceable animals and ends with a vision of a garden restored, complete with crystalline river and prolific trees.

For Christians, the inner link of protology and eschatology, the organic movement from beginnings to ends, is rooted in the fundamentals of our faith. Christians confess that God is Triune, which is as much as to say that in God there is not only a "beginning," the Father, but also an "ending," a product, the

1

Son, begotten by the Spirit. The Son is irreducibly different from the Father, as different from the Father as ends are from beginnings. Yet the Son is also the exact image of the Father, so that in seeing the Son one can see the Father. Between this Beginning and the End, nothing leaks out or is wasted. All that the Father is, the Son is, except that the Father is Beginning and the Son End.

At a different register, Christians confess that the Son is Himself Beginning and End. He is the "first-born" of the Father, the Father's first and unique Word, who was with the Father from the beginning. Yet He is also the final Word, the Judge appointed by the Father who will, at the very last, tell us what it was all about and reveal once and for all who wore the white hats, and who the black hats, and who the black hats painted white. Christ is the first letter and the last, the Alpha and the Omega, in the alphabet that is human history.

That is not quite right. Creation does not circle back to square one. The story of the Bible is not a circle, but a history of creation in development, creation becoming. It is the history of a garden growing up to be a garden city that is also a bride. Along with the trees and river of Revelation 21-22, there are walls and streets and nations hauling in their treasures. The biblical story is not merely creation and return, not merely beginning, loss, and recovery of beginning. Scripture tells a story of creation's glorification.

And that too, unthinkably, is rooted in Triune life. The Father is wholly God, but He is also, mysteriously,

"more" by begetting a Son than He would be otherwise. He has, of course, always had that Son; the Son
is, as Athanasius says, "proper" to the Father's essence,
and the begetting of the Son is an eternal begetting.
The Father has eternally been "more." We might put it
this way: The Triune God is not so much a timeless
God as a God who has always already realized His
future. He is the Alpha that has always already been,
equally and simultaneously, Omega. He is the
infinitely productive seed that is always already
eternally tree and fruit.

Press our two main observations together, and we
get to the premise of Mike Bull's remarkable *Bible
Matrix*. On the one hand, the Bible's beginnings are
the seeds from which the rest of the Bible grows; on the
other hand, the Bible's story is one of glorification. If
both are true, then we should expect to find, within
the Bible's beginnings, hints of the story of glorification that reaches its end in the New Jerusalem. In the
Alpha words of Genesis 1, we should be able to discern
some clues to the Omega words of the Apocalypse.

And so we do. Each day of creation week is an
advance over the last. That there is anything—even a
dark, formless emptiness, or empty formlessness—that
is other than God is a remarkable enough fact by itself
(Genesis 1:2). But on Day 1, Yahweh determines that
the world needs light, and over the subsequent days,
He speaks the world into shape and fills it with all
manner of delightful clutter. Yahweh will move the
world along and make it better along the way. We
know that because that is how the story starts. From

the seed of the beginning, we form a nascent sense of what the full plant will look like.

This insight is the heart of *Bible Matrix*. Mike Bull does more than show us the big story of the Bible, the movement from glorious beginning to the greater glory of the end. That is a story so obvious that even academic Bible scholars can see it. But Bull sees what few have seen, namely, that this big story is present seminally in the opening chapter of the Bible, and more than that, that the glorification of the world is not only the big story of Scripture but also the shape of nearly every little story of the Bible as well. Seed, tree, and every leaf and branch of the tree, is imprinted with the same Triune pattern.

Bible Matrix connects pieces of the Bible that might have looked like scattered fragments. It shows coherence and recurring sequences where you might have seen only randomness and confusion. It gives the world in a grain of sand, as Bull explains how each passage and portion of the Bible is a lens through which the whole is uniquely refracted. Bull roots around in the genetics of Scripture and everywhere discovers not a circle of identical return but the chiastically coiled DNA that moves creation from glory to glory.

My hope is that *Bible Matrix* will itself be a seed, and that its creative and arresting insights will burrow down into the souls of readers until they germinate and begin, by the power of the Spirit, to produce the fruit of a transformed, biblical imagination.

1

BIG BIBLE HANDLE

THE BIBLE IS A VERY STRANGE BOOK TO MODERN MINDS. Even the passages we know very well contain a great number of oddities and we allow them to grow familiar without gaining an understanding of why they are there.

Those brave enough to regularly read the Old Testament often find themselves wondering what on earth is going on. *"Just keep reading your Bible"* our pastors tell us. Do you ever get the feeling they don't have a big grip on it either? *"Just stick to the basics. The rest doesn't matter."*

A few years ago, I discovered the not-very-well-known theologian James B. Jordan. I didn't understand everything he said, but I did realize that this was partly because he spoke just like the Bible: matter-of-fact, flesh-and-blood, and every now and then, outright *bizarre*.

He got me thinking, and I found that even the most curious things he spoke of became continuous threads. Jordan identifies what he calls the "universals"— themes that are repeated, not unlike a musical motif. After listening to many of his lectures, I began to recognize these themes myself, much as you would recognize the signature music when a hero or villain appears once again in a movie. Except the Bible does it *a lot better.*

The most amazing discovery, to me, was Jordan's understanding of the Creation Week as a common literary structure in the Bible. There is no better way to research something than to write a book about it, so I started one. I intended to show how this 7-point pattern structured the major events of the Bible. I got to Abraham and found that the pattern was operating not only at a grand, over-arching level but also at levels *within* the larger cycles. And all in perfect harmony.

This incredible structuring means that the Bible is a "fractal," a rough geometrical shape that can be split into parts, each of which is a smaller version of the whole.

Although the Bible's literature often appears disorganized to us, it has in fact been *extremely carefully crafted.* Yet for the last hundred years or so, many scholars have treated the Scriptures as a shoddy, primitive jumble.

Analysis of the Bible's literary structures has proven these scholars wrong. It has shown that this Book is *smarter than we are.* We have been harsh critics of something we didn't understand—like drinkers of cheap beer ridiculing the wine fair.

Now, before you class me with the people who spend their time searching for hidden codes in the Bible (often while they calmly ignore its very clear and intended messages), this renewed interest in literary structure has some very solid benefits for Christians. This is not about hunting for mysterious patterns; it is about learning how to read the Bible in the way it was meant to be read.

THE BIG HANDLE

Ever wish someone could give you a big handle on the whole Bible without years of study? You pick up *that* Christian book and think, "Ah, I've finally found the answer!" only to be bombarded with an endless stream of data to assimilate. All you discovered was that the more we know, the more we realize we don't know.

Well, this book not only promises to give you that big handle—*it will deliver on the promise.* Yes, you will realize how much you don't know, but you will have such a handle on God's way of communicating, and on the big picture of Bible history, that you will be able to approach and study any passage with confidence.

You should be asking, *how is this possible?* The Bible is one story told over and over again, with many variations on the same theme. The variations are based on Genesis chapter 1 (expanded upon in chapters 2-3), so they all follow a similar structure. This underlying framework is the skeleton key that opens all the doors.

I believe that much of the misinterpretation that causes Christian scholars to disagree can be avoided if we identify the use of this elementary pattern—the Bible's DNA. This field is not something to be reserved for the mystic fringe (although such people are more used to thinking in this way). God's work is both marvelously engineered and ravishingly artistic. He is not the author of confusion.

When we learn to recognize the shape of God's sovereign work in the past, it enables us to understand how He is working in the present and how He will work in the future. God is bringing His people to maturity on every level. It becomes clear that our personal temptations and sufferings are significant because they bear the same signature as the histories of families, churches, nations and empires.

BIBLICAL THEOLOGY

A young Christian friend recently said to me, "You know, I just don't get the Old Testament." If we are honest with ourselves, we don't either. A process called *biblical theology* will help us. It is the "big picture" process.

There are two basic theological methods. **Systematic theology** disassembles the Bible like *Lego* bricks and puts all the same colored bricks together in little plastic boxes (like many of those Christian books you have read).

It is a necessary process, but if that is all we do, we underestimate the powerful, carefully-crafted literature these "bricks" were removed from. Like coals abstracted from a mesmerizing fire, they soon become lifeless objects devoid of personality.

Biblical theology, however, is very different. It is like watching *all* the coals in the fire. It is like listening to a symphony and noticing the repeated themes (both how they are similar and how they have been altered). It enables you to analyze both the obvious and the more subtle ways in which the composer is communicating his message. It interprets the living Scriptures *organically.*

All those separate *Lego* bricks are part of a composition that links them together. The Bible uses a repertoire of repeated symbols, and the symbols describe the relationship of one "brick" to another.

For instance, when Satan is referred to as a *serpent,* he is using the weapon of deceit. When he is a *dragon,* he is persecuting and devouring. In Revelation 12, he is a serpent to the Woman but a dragon to her children—all in the same passage.

Very often, a Bible brick has greater meaning when observed in relationship to other bricks. Indeed, sometimes this is the *only* way it has meaning. *Symbols are relationships.*

In context, as part of a story instead of an item on a boring list, these elements are also easier to remember.

The Bible is like the Bayeux Tapestry, a long-running account of God's people in history. Sadly, many modern conservative scholars prefer to spend their time squabbling over the mass of threads on the back of the cloth, all the while ignoring the exhilarating *big picture* on the front. They are technicians who see and record dots. To be fully understood, the Bible also requires artists who are able to "join the dots."

While the academies, when it all boils down, have their students getting to know everything about the Bible but the Bible itself, is it any wonder many teachers are inept when it comes to communicating its big picture to their churches? Is it any wonder that most

Christians are biblically illiterate and have to spend money on books—sometimes very suspect books—to tell them what the Bible says?

Biblical theology should be taught to *everyone* in church for three good reasons:

1 *We don't know how to read the Bible.* We need to interpret it properly before we can apply it. We forget we are reading someone else's mail, and take it out of context. We apply texts directly to ourselves or to current newspaper headlines with disastrous results. When we meet together, we search our feelings or latch onto any old idea we find rattling around in our subconscious, pool our ignorance and claim we are taking the Bible at "face value." *We wouldn't treat any other literature this way.* Who was it written to? What events were on their horizon? What previous events could the author be referring to? Where does the passage fit in history? What previous history does the text have in Scripture? Without checking for "previous," we have no frame of reference for our interpretation of a passage before we make an application of its truth.

2 *We ignore or isolate the Old Testament.* We stay in safe, familiar territory, which leaves most of the Bible unexplored and foreign to us. And when we do deal with the Old Testament, it is presented as disconnected morality tales rather than as waves in an increasing conquest. This leaves Christians without a clue about how God works in history. We also fail to see Christ predicted throughout all the

Old Covenant Scriptures. This is bigger than a "Where's Waldo" hunt for Jesus. There are recurring event-patterns and symbols that must be observed if we are to understand the structure of Jesus' ministry, the goal of the Great Commission and the history of the first-century church.

3 *We misinterpret much of the New Testament,* including some of its key passages, because we are ignorant of how God's plan unfolded in the Old Testament. To interpret the last chapter of a book, you must understand everything that has gone before. For instance, understanding that the "Restoration" period laid the foundation for the events of the first century is the only way to interpret the "apocalyptic" passages of the New Testament successfully.[1]

All this brings us to the most important point of this introduction: the Bible's use of symbols—*typology.*

SYMBOLISM

The Bible's symbolism is based on the fact that everything made by God has a message. All matter is like wax stamped with God's seal, and all the elements of Creation say something about the nature of their Creator.

Like anything made today—especially clothing—Creation has a logo stamped on it. *God's logo is Man.* Man is the primary symbol that points to God. That

---

1 The "Restoration era" began with Israel's release from captivity under Babylonian rule and ended in the first century.

pointing has been corrupted by sin, and Christ came to be a perfect logo and then restore the logo in us. He is the Word, and by His Creative Spirit, He makes us Words.

The Greek word for a stamp or pattern is *typos*, which is where we get *type*face and *type*writer from. So the study of symbols and patterns in the Bible is called **Typology**.

Typology is a large part of biblical theology—I think the most exciting. Due to past abuses, it is currently unpopular. However, the Bible cannot be fully understood without allowing this upper layer of predictive symbolism to have its place in our thinking.

For sure, anything we want to see can be read into literature, and the fear of the "minimalists" is that if this door is opened, the Scriptures will be misused and our minds will be filled with crazy ideas.

But with this door shut, even the scholars are often unable to make much sense of numerous passages. They have banned driving because some people went off-road.

Is typology really that dangerous? Are there any built-in restraints on its abuse? James Jordan writes:

"Some [Old Testament] events are clearly and pointedly symbolic and typological, while some are only vaguely and generally so. We have to explain this in order to distance ourselves from the 'interpretive minimalism' that has come to characterize evangelical commentaries on Scripture in recent years. We do not need some specific New Testament verse to 'prove' that a

12

given Old Testament story has symbolic dimensions. Rather, such symbolic dimensions are presupposed in the very fact that man is the image of God. Thus, we ought not be afraid to hazard a guess at the wider prophetic meanings of Scripture narratives, as we consider how they image the ways of God.

Such a 'maximalist' approach as this puts us more in line with the kind of interpretation used by the Church Fathers. It seems dangerous, because it is not readily evident what kinds of checks and balances are to be employed in such an approach. Do the five loaves and two fishes represent the five books of Moses and the Old and New Testaments? Almost certainly not. What, however, is our check on such an interpretation? We have to say that the check and balance on interpretation is the whole rest of Scripture and of theology. As time goes along, and we learn more and more, our interpretations will become refined. If we do not plunge in and try now, however, that day of refinement will never come."[2]

There are two main "checks and balances" that restrain us from misusing the Bible's symbols. The first is the Bible's **consistent use** of the same symbols. There is a verse in John Newton's hymn *Amazing Grace* which makes me cringe, because it describes God's mercy as a *flood* and the end of the world as being like dissolving

---

2 James B. Jordan, *Judges: God's War Against Humanism,* pp. xii-xiii.

snow. I love that hymn, but I know the Bible only uses a flood symbol to describe the *destruction* of unfaithful Covenant people, and snow is always, somehow, related to *righteousness.*

Secondly, the symbols are most often contained in the **repeated event-patterns** which structure the Bible. In other words, the symbols know their place. To goad those too timid to venture beyond *Lego* brick systematic theology, I like to call this *systematic typology.* It is symbols contained in a repeated structure, like seven powerlines running right through the Bible, with each occurrence of the pattern as the power pole that holds them in place and in order. The repeated structure is what allows us to make and *verify* the typological connections between the events described.

Of course, each occurrence is not identical. The common pattern is refracted in a myriad of different ways. To illustrate this, imagine a dinner set where every patterned dinner plate has a piece missing. If we stack all of the plates, carefully lining up the corresponding bits of the pattern we do have, it is very likely we will be able to see the complete pattern using all the incomplete plates. This is exactly how the Bible is constructed. Although the first "plate," Genesis 1-3, is extremely brief, it contains the seeds of the rest of the Bible in breathtaking potency. This primeval word takes on "flesh" as the pattern is replayed throughout Bible history.

The most basic event-structure is the Creation narrative in Genesis 1, and it is the chord from which the entire Bible "symphony" flows. When you see a passage that recapitulates the Creation Week, there are some very valid things you can draw from the text that aren't actually *written* in it. This is a subtle element of Scripture that many bright scholars refuse to see.

Genesis 1 is the Bible Matrix. As it matures throughout the Scriptures, the identification of this pattern unlocks the books of Moses, Israel's history, the structure of Jesus' ministry and the book of Revelation. If the Bible is truly God's Word, *should we expect anything less?* It also has staggering implications concerning the identity, purpose and future of Christianity—and these implications are thoroughly, joyously liberating.

THINKING GOD'S THOUGHTS

One reason we have a hard time understanding the Bible is because we keep imposing our modern world views onto it. The Bible speaks its own language. It comes in like a sword and violates our thinking until we think the way God does. God does not speak in theological jargon or ideology divorced from reality. He speaks in the energizing, intoxicating flesh-and-blood symbols of the Creation, *and so should we.*

This book draws a great deal upon the genius of theologians James B. Jordan and Peter J. Leithart.[3] These bold, godly, good-humored men have answered questions I have had for many years. I can honestly say that, due to their influence, I look at the Bible in a

---

3 See *Recommended Reading and Listening* on page 223.

totally different way. I can open it to any book now and feel completely at home, even if I haven't studied that book in detail. This is because I now recognize the furniture.

Bible Matrix is an introduction to the interpretive method used in my Bible commentary, *Totus Christus: A Biblical Theology of the Whole Christ*, which also summarizes a great deal of Jordan and Leithart's groundbreaking work.

Once you get a handle on this method, I recommend taking the next step with that commentary and seeing these structures—and their exciting implications—in much greater detail.

But I have no doubt that this introduction is more than enough to get you understanding the Bible in a much deeper way, all on your own. And I can assure you, it is *mind-blowing*. You will never look at the Bible—or the world—in quite the same way again.

You take the blue pill, the story ends, you wake up in your bed and believe whatever you want to believe.
You take the red pill, you stay in Wonderland, and I show you how deep the rabbit hole goes...

Remember, all I am offering is the truth. Nothing more.

No one can be told what the Matrix is. You have to see it for yourself.

—Morpheus, to Neo, in *The Matrix*

WHAT IS
A MATRIX?

ma·trix

Etymology:

Latin, female animal used for breeding, parent plant, from matr-, mater

Date: 1555

1 something within or from which something else originates, develops, or takes form

2 a: a mold from which a relief surface (as a piece of type) is made

b: an engraved or inscribed die or stamp

c: an electroformed impression of a phonograph record used for mass-producing duplicates of the original

3 a: the natural material (as soil or rock) in which something (as a fossil or crystal) is embedded

b: material in which something is enclosed or embedded (as for protection or study)

TYPOLOGY

The Greek word typos refers to an image impressed onto something else, for instance, wax. It is the word used in Scripture for the imprint of God's heavenly pattern on the earth, and thus it is absolutely fundamental to a biblical worldview.

In Acts 7:44 Stephen says, "Our fathers had the Tabernacle of testimony in the wilderness, just as He who spoke to Moses directed him to make it according to the pattern [type] which he had seen." Similarly, Hebrews 8:5, quoting Exodus 25:40, reminds us that Moses was told, "See that you make all things according to the pattern [type] which was shown you on the mountain."

As we have seen, there is a succession of such imprints. Each imprint is more glorious than the one before. Solomon's Temple was more glorious than the Mosaic Tabernacle.

Ezekiel's visionary Temple (Ezekiel 40-48) was more glorious than Solomon's Temple. The New Jerusalem is more glorious yet.

The study of how each of these models is transformed into the next, and the parallels between them, is part of typology.

Because all men are made in the image of God, all men bear His imprint. Every man is, thus, in one sense a type of every other man. More importantly, church leaders are to be types or models for kingdom citizens (Philippians 1:7; 1 Thessalonians 1:7; 1 Timothy 4:12; Titus 2:7; 1 Peter 5:3). In terms of a typological view of history, the kingdom of men in the Old Covenant was a type of the New Covenant (1 Corinthians 10:6, 11), and the first Adam was a type of the Last (Romans 5:14).

A great deal of nonsense has been published under the banner of typology; but in spite of this, the fact remains that typology is the fundamental biblical philosophy of history. Typology means that history is under God's control, not man's. It means that the successive stages of world history have meaning, a meaning related to the heavenly pattern and God's purpose to glorify man and the world progressively.

James B. Jordan, *Through New Eyes, Developing a Biblical View of the World*, pp. 49-50.

2

FLYING INFORMATION

THE NEXT FEW CHAPTERS ARE LIKE FLYING LESSONS. You are going to learn to think in new ways, to see the Bible—and the world—with an extra dimension usually reserved for poets, madmen and the authors of the Scriptures.

If you find you are not getting it, don't worry. You may be someone *visual,* like me, who learns better by seeing things in action, and there will be plenty of action shortly. If you are non-visual, I advise you to repress the urge to demand a full engineering report on this bumblebee before you see it do the physically impossible and fly. And I can tell you from experience, this thing flies with the mighty wings of a four-faced cherubim.

LEARNING BIBLE PATTERNS

There are three fundamental seven-step patterns in Scripture, which are often three strands of the same cord.

The first is the seven day **Creation** pattern, which appears sometimes as *con*-struction and sometimes as *de*-struction.

The second, and most important, is the **Dominion**

pattern, which is repeated many times in the Old Testament and is also the deep structure of the New. It marks out and claims the territory promised to us by God as a new creation.

The third is the pattern of the seven **Festivals** given to the nation of Israel. These feasts show us that the process of gathering God's people is written into Creation as the harvest year.

You Christians who know the Bible will begin to recognize these patterns in passages that are very familiar. They have already become part of your subconscious, and this is the purpose for which they were designed. The Bible recasts the shape of the way we *think* in order to forge the shape of the way we *live*. Meditating on these patterns and their implications has given me a bigger handle on the Scriptures. It has also given the Scriptures a bigger handle on me.

Understanding the Bible requires a biblical theology that is not only literary and historical but also *typological*. This extra dimension is not optional but crucial. This is how Christ has revealed Himself.

There's no need for any obscure Scriptures to remain as isolated parts of a mystery antique. In fact, when understood in both their historical context and literary structure, these can be the most rewarding. Not a word is idle. The Bible is absolute perfection, an unfathomably integrated living organism, and the literary architecture of a growing house, head and body—the *Whole Christ*.

PERFECT SYMMETRY

HAVE YOU EVER WONDERED why there is repetition in many passages of Scripture? The Bible often uses a literary structure much like a flock of geese flying in formation. The geese on each end are corresponding events, and each goose corresponds to its counterpart until we reach the central point, which is often the main message of the passage—the *thesis*. A seven-fold (heptamerous) formation would look like this:

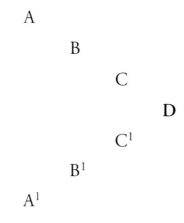

A and A^1 are related ideas, if not identical. A^1 is often an expansion of A, and B^1 of B, etc. The pattern is known as a *chiasm* (ky-azm). Chiasms are common throughout Scripture.

The Bible is neither an archaic shambles nor a *linear* torrent of data to be absorbed and merely "systematized." As we shall see, it is literary **architecture**. To be interpreted it must be read in *three dimensions*.

COMMENTS

Here is a basic chiasm from 2 Samuel. Not only can we observe that God is totally in control of history, but also that the author of this text has crafted it as carefully as God crafted the history.

2 | FLYING INFORMATION

A Chiasm:
The Bathsheba Narrative

A Joab is on the field besieging Rabbah, but David has stayed behind in Jerusalem (2 Samuel 11:1)

  B David sleeps with Bathsheba, and she becomes pregnant (11:2-5)

    C David arranges for Uriah's death (11:6-25)

      D Bathsheba mourns for Uriah (11:26-27)

        E Nathan confronts David's sin (12:1-15a)

      D¹David mourns for his infant son (12:15b-17)

    C¹David's son dies (12:18-23)

  B¹David sleeps with Bathsheba, and she becomes pregnant (12:24-25)

A¹David goes to Rabbah and finishes the siege, then returns to Jerusalem (12:26-31)[1]

---

1 From Peter J. Leithart, *A House For My Name,* p. 150.

METHOD IN THE MADNESS

Chiastic structures were a means of ordering information so it could be remembered easily. Since literacy was limited, literature was designed to be read aloud and *heard*. In the preface to his book, *The Literary Structure of the Old Testament*, David Dorsey writes:

> "My fascination with [Hebrew literary structure] was kindled when I began teaching Old Testament courses in seminary. At that time I was struck by the apparent lack of order within many of the biblical books. Jeremiah seemed hopelessly confused in its organization; so did Isaiah and Hosea and most of the prophets. Song of Songs and Ecclesiastes appeared to be in almost complete disarray, and even the more orderly historical books, such as Joshua and Kings, showed signs of strangely careless organization.
>
> Why did the biblical authors write like this? I would never write a book, an article, or even a private letter with such carelessness of arrangement. I was intrigued by the possibility that the Hebrew authors might have organized their compositions according to literary conventions that were different from ours.
>
> I began to discover, over a period of years, that several structuring patterns rarely used by us were remarkably common in the books of the Hebrew Bible, particularly chiasmus (symmetry), parallelism, and sevenfold patterns. I was increasingly

struck by how often these patterns had been utilized to arrange biblical books...

It was my mother who gave me a love for literature. She read to my brother Stephen and me regularly, from as early as I can remember. I still have many fond memories of those wondrous bedtime stories, whose structures—like the Bible—were designed for the ear, not the eye."

Besides symmetries and parallelisms, there are those three basic patterns in the Bible: Creation, Festivals and Dominion. These may take a little time to get a grip on, but like learning to ride a bicycle, this is the hardest part of the process. Once you get a handle on it, you can go anywhere.

3

DOMINION

THE MOST IMPORTANT HISTORICAL STRUCTURE is the Dominion pattern. Although it is chiastic, it also **progresses** from *Creation* to *Glorification,* from childhood to maturity. As a chiasm, it leaves the house and returns home, but like the lost son in Luke 15, its culmination is the reward of a hard-won wisdom. Here is the seven-point pattern at its basic level:

1	CREATION
2	*Division*
3	*Ascension*
4	**Testing**
5	*Maturity*
6	*Conquest*
7	GLORIFICATION

Later, we will see how this process is also symmetrical (chiastic) through the common elements in *Creation* and *Glorification,* in *Division* and *Conquest,* and in *Ascension* and *Maturity.*

This structure is written into our lives at many levels. *Creation* is the "word" or event that initiates a situation. At *Division,* the "word" begins to alter the world somehow. *Ascension* brings the situation to a head—some sort of conflict that must be resolved. *Testing* is where the implications of the conflict are fully understood, and people are forced to take the side of good or of evil. At *Maturity,* the underdogs muster themselves in preparation for the final battle. After their *Conquest,* they receive the prize at *Glorification.* Because this structure is the DNA of the Bible—the book that founded our culture—you will see that it underlies many, even most, novels and movies.

This structure also reflects God's pattern for a Christian life. We are born, come to faith, learn about God, are tested and matured, gain wisdom, are resurrected and finally glorified to rule with God. Even if mankind had not fallen into sin, there still would have been this process of planting, watering, growth, pruning, harvest, gathering and feasting with God for every man.

The purpose of identifying this pattern in the Scriptures is not to ignore their obvious message in favor of a hidden one. It is a foundation for interpreting them correctly so we can better *understand* the temptation and suffering we experience, and better *obey* God's glorious purposes for us in Christ.

Creation - **God gives life to a man**

Division - **The man is set apart for service**

Ascension - **God brings him near and gives him a mission**

Testing - **His loyalty to God is tested**

Maturity - **If successful, the man is rewarded with plunder**

Conquest - **The man appears before God again**

Glorification - **God gives rest to the man. Because he was faithful, God also gives him greater authority**

COMMENTS

This might seem a lot like a grand quest, but in fact it is the structure God has built into every day of human life...

Creation - **You wake from sleep**

Division - **You go to work**

Ascension - **You are given instructions**

Testing - **You work unsupervised. Your faculties are tested**

Maturity - **The work brings you prosperity and wisdom**

Conquest - **You return home**

Glorification - **You eat and rest**

COMMENTS

Death and resurrection are thus built into every "evening and morning." Notice that every normal human day is basically chiastic.

Over time, your faithfulness brings you promotion, with greater wealth and authority. This is God's way of giving gradual dominion of the world to His people.

DOMINION PATTERN IN THE EXODUS

- *Creation* - God calls a people through Moses the **mediator**

- *Division* - As a **people**, they are set apart and escape through the waters of the Red Sea (**death**)

- *Ascension* - Moses draws near to God and receives His **Law**. The Lord makes a new Covenant with His people

- *Testing* - Through **trials** in the wilderness, Israel is threshed; sin is judged in the light of the new Law

- *Maturity* - The traitors and fearful pass away, a new army is mustered, and the **Law** is repeated

- *Conquest* - As an **army**, they cross through the waters of the Jordan River (**resurrection**)

- *Glorification* - The new nation defeats and rules over the old nations, acting as **corporate mediator** between God and men

COMMENTS

The most helpful appearance of this pattern in the Bible is the Exodus of Israel under Moses and their entry into Canaan under Joshua. Memorize this chart and you will have a solid basis for understanding all the others.
Notice the symmetry of the concepts in **bold**.

DOMINION PATTERN IN
GENESIS TO JUDGES

The first seven books of the Bible follow this pattern, with a growth into maturity from children to wise *Judges,* who are by definition "mature... hav(ing) their powers of discernment trained *by constant practice* to distinguish good from evil" (Hebrews 5:14). This was God's plan for Adam and is the climax of God's plan for mankind. He seeks "godly offspring" (Malachi 2:15).

Genesis - God *creates* a people through the patriarchs (Abraham, Isaac, Jacob and Joseph)

> **Exodus** - Under Moses, He *separates* a new people to Himself

>> **Leviticus** - He institutes a new priesthood, and tells them what is required by **Law** to *draw near* to His throne

>>> **Numbers** - The children of Israel are *tested* as they travel through the wilderness

>>> **Deuteronomy**[1] - Moses repeats the **Law** to the next generation *assembled before him*

>> **Joshua** - With Joshua as Captain (head), the people (body) enter fully into God's promises

> **Judges** - Israel rules over the new Land that God had promised them. In this case, they mostly fail miserably and a new beginning is required

COMMENTS

___

In the book of Judges, we read that even though Israel was given victory and rulership over Canaan, they failed to maintain dominion. A new cycle was required. But for now, the point is about God's intention: the process is supposed to make us wise, like Solomon, able to judge correctly between good and evil.

1 Deuteronomy means "Second Law."

4

FESTIVALS

GUESS WHAT? The nation of Israel had seven feasts, and they follow the same pattern. They are outlined in Leviticus 23.

These festivals portray Dominion as a **harvest**. They show us that the process of freeing, purifying and gathering God's people is written into Creation as the harvest year.

So we see the same progression from *Creation* to *Glorification* in Israel's annual calendar.

LEVITICUS 23: ANNUAL FEASTS

Creation - **Sabbath** - God's rest

Division - **Passover** - *Sin removed*

Ascension - **Firstfruits** - Brought to God

Testing - **Pentecost** - *LAW REVEALED*

Maturity - **Trumpets** - Brought to God

Conquest - **Atonement** - *Sin removed*

Glorification - **Booths** - Man's rest

COMMENTS

For the redeemed slaves, the process began with the weekly festival, a perfect Creation Week, as the microcosmic source of the festive year.

If we align the festivals on this page with the Dominion pattern on the next page, the symmetry in the festivals' fundamental purposes correlates with the bringing of God's people from Egypt to Canaan.

We can identify Moses as the **Firstfruits** offering, the beginning of the first generation harvest (**Pentecost**), and the later generation as the final harvest of olives and grapes in the Promised Land (**Booths**).

DOMINION PATTERN IN THE EXODUS

Creation - God calls a people through Moses the **mediator**

Division - As a **people**, they are set apart and escape through the waters of the Red Sea (**death**)

Ascension - Moses draws near to God and receives His **Law**. The Lord makes a new Covenant with His people

Testing - Through **trials** in the wilderness, Israel is threshed; sin is judged in the light of the new Law

Maturity - The traitors and fearful pass away, a new army is mustered, and the **Law** is repeated

Conquest - As an **army**, they cross through the waters of the Jordan river (**resurrection**)

Glorification - The new nation defeats and rules over the old nations, acting as **corporate mediator** between God and men

 COMMENTS

Notice that the Law received by Moses was what tested—"threshed"—the Hebrews in the wilderness.

Details of these feasts follow on the next two pages. They seem strange to modern people, but this process is the key to many Bible passages.

41

GOD'S REST

Creation - **Sabbath**
(Leviticus 23:1-3)
The beginning of a new creation. A weekly rest that sets the pattern for the greater annual one.

SIN REMOVED

Division - **Passover**
(Leviticus 23:4-8)
At midnight, an animal's blood is a covering—a firmament—for sin.

BROUGHT TO GOD

Ascension - **Firstfruits**
(Leviticus 23:9-14)
The beginning of the grain harvest.

LAW REVEALED

Testing - **Pentecost**
(Leviticus 23:15-22)
The grain is harvested and threshed.

BROUGHT TO GOD

Maturity - **Trumpets**
(Leviticus 23:23-25)
The nation is summoned to God for judgment. The soldiers demonstrate their commitment by paying a specified price for the privilege.

SIN REMOVED

> *Conquest -* **Atonement** *(Coverings)*
> (Leviticus 23:26-32)
> *The people fast. Wearing linen instead of
> his usual glorious robes, the High Priest
> sacrifices a bull for his own sins, and a lot
> is drawn (the Lord chooses) for one of two
> goats to be sacrificed for the sins of the
> people. Their blood is sprinkled seven
> times before the Ark in the Most Holy
> Place—in the dark. The sins are spoken
> over the other goat, which is sent into the
> wilderness to its death.*

MAN'S REST

> *Glorification -* **Booths** *(Ingathering)*
> (Leviticus 23:33-43)
> *Grapes and olives are harvested. The people
> feast. They live in booths made of branches
> and remember their deliverance from
> Egypt. Gentiles are invited to celebrate
> with them.*

COMMENTS

At **Trumpets**, the "army" was presented before God and
all those over twenty years of age paid for the privilege.
For God, the second generation that came out of the
wilderness *was* the plunder. This "resurrected" Israel
was an army leaving boot camp.

Notice that there is symmetry in the blood of
Passover and the blood of **Atonement**.

5

CREATION

WE HAVE COVERED Dominion and Festivals. Now it's time to see how those are based on the Creation Week in Genesis 1.

COMMENTS

There were three days of forming new "empty spaces" by dividing the original watery deep (the Abyss), then three days of filling them.

- The heavens of Day 1 were filled on Day 4.
- The sky and sea of Day 2 were filled on Day 5.
- The Land of Day 3 was filled on Day 6.

1	▶	4
2	▶	5
3	▶	6

Notice that both Day 1 and Day 4 concern light. Day 1 is singular, and Day 4 is plural. The first is the "head" (king), and the fourth is the "body" (government of elders).

Notice also the preliminary filling at the end of Day 3, with the grain and fruit plants filling the Land as a promise of the Sabbath table of Day 7 (bread and wine). Day 3 corresponds to **Firstfruits**, and Day 7 to the big feast at **Booths**.

Day 5 concerns swarms. It is about bands of brothers, armies and plagues. The clouds of incense picture multitudes of men as God's government, mature elders prepared as a robe for the Lord.

Adam's creation corresponds to the High Priest on the **Day of Atonement**.

The odd one out seems to be Day 4. Adam is tested under God's Law. The sun, moon and five visible planets correspond to the seven "governing" lights of the Lampstand. The Tabernacle follows the same pattern because God's house is a new Creation. We will discuss this later on.

GENESIS 1: THE CREATION WEEK

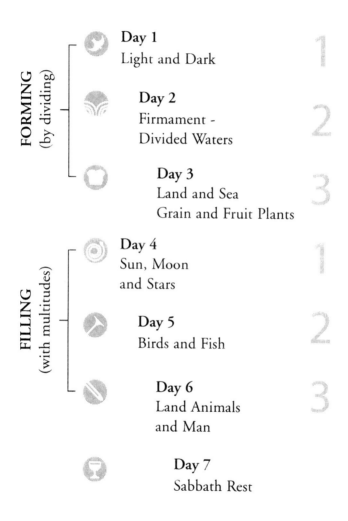

FORMING (by dividing)

Day 1
Light and Dark

1

Day 2
Firmament -
Divided Waters

2

Day 3
Land and Sea
Grain and Fruit Plants

3

FILLING (with multitudes)

Day 4
Sun, Moon
and Stars

1

Day 5
Birds and Fish

2

Day 6
Land Animals
and Man

3

Day 7
Sabbath Rest

Corresponding the Creation Days with the Dominion and Festivals patterns might seem to be too much of a mental stretch at this early stage, so I will reassure you once again: when you see this glorious triple-braided process in action, it will all begin to fall into place.

6

NEW CREATION MATRIX

WHAT YOU WILL SEE NEXT is the complete structure God uses in all His dealings with His Creation. In this final chart, all three patterns correspond—**Creation, Feasts** and **Dominion**.[1]

Every time a pattern is repeated, some extra aspects are highlighted. In any given cycle, one pattern may be dominant, but all three are still present and shed light on each other.

This structure is the heartbeat of the Creation. It is the cycle of a human day and a human life. It is the pattern of the Tabernacle. It is the process of agriculture. It undergirds the speeches and Laws of God. It orders the rise and fall of nations and empires. As we will see, it is also the structure of our worship. It is the rhythm of Christ.

---

1 More advanced readers of theology might appreciate that these three patterns constitute Word, Sacrament and Government.

COMMENTS

I suggest you take ten minutes to study this page and let it sink in. You might even begin to recognize this pattern in some Bible passages you know well. One I would point out is that after the *Ascension* of Christ, the Holy Spirit appeared over the saints as tongues of fire. They became the Lampstand at **Pentecost**.

Things might seem to be getting a little complicated now, but don't worry. These patterns are repeated so many times in the Bible that, as we see them in various passages of Scripture, they will become second nature to you. And you can always refer back to these early chapters if necessary.

Plus, we will give this a practice run to demonstrate how it works.

Creation	Dominion	Feasts
Day 1 Light - Night & Day *(Ark of the Covenant)*	**Genesis** *Creation*	**Sabbath** (promise of rest) *God's rest*
Day 2 Waters divided *(Veil)*	**Exodus** *Division*	**Passover** (sin covered) *Adam's sin removed*
Day 3 Dry Land, Grain & Fruit *(Altar & Table)*	**Leviticus** *Ascension*	**Firstfruits** (priesthood) *Adam brought to God*
Day 4 Ruling Lights *(Lampstand)*	**Numbers** *Testing*	**Pentecost** (harvest) *Law revealed*
Day 5 Birds & Fish *(Incense Altar)*	**Deuteronomy** *Maturity*	**Trumpets** (armies) *Eve brought to God*
Day 6 Animals & Man *(Mediators: High)* *Priest & Sacrifices)*	**Joshua** *Conquest*	**Atonement** (sin expelled) *Eve removed from sin*
Day 7 Rest & Ruling *(Shekinah Glory)*	**Judges** *Glorification*	**Booths** (ingathering) *Adam's rest*

Tool Kit

I know this is a deluge of information. It is a lot to digest and internalize, so here I summarize what motifs and symbols to look out for as an aid to identifying and verifying this structure. Remember, all three patterns are tied together, and in any occurrence, one in particular will usually shine more than the others.

It is also a great help to remember that this pattern is a process initiated by a Word from the Lord (or His prophet) that brings about a creative (or destructive) change to move history forward. It moves His people (as children) to greater maturity and greater authority.

Again, for those readers willing to suspend their judgment and keep reading, don't stress too much about remembering these details for now. As mentioned earlier, observing these elements as parts of a structure is far more memorable than systematizing them. Seeing them in action makes their rhythm familiar.

Creation

This step always concerns the initiating "Word" from God to man. It is the light on Day 1 of Creation, the Tablets hidden in the Ark. Sometimes it is a stagnated Sabbath rest (like slavery in Egypt) that the Lord comes to disturb with a new cycle so a better rest may be given. Cycles often begin with someone speaking.

Division

At this step you will find the firmament, a robe, or something torn in two. It is the dark heavens as a garment—the Tabernacle veil. Sometimes there is sackcloth as a symbol of mourning for sin or the tearing of a robe as a symbol of grief. All this is the death in the darkness of the Passover. It is a people torn in two by the sword of the Creative Word. Here, you will also find a journey, an exodus of those called at the *Creation* step to *divide* from those who are not called.

Ascension

Ascension concerns the Covenant "head." It is fundamentally "singular." This is the firstfruits of the harvest. It is Moses ascending Sinai to receive the Law. As Day 3, the Bronze Altar is the mountain rising out of the sea, and Moses is the new Adam submitting to God as grain and fruit plants, a promise of future bread and wine, the Table of Showbread ("bread of the face"). The new Covenant made at *Ascension* is a "betrothal" promise to be consummated, fulfilled at *Glorification*.

Part of this "nearbringing of Adam" (as High Priest) at *Ascension* was the institution of a centralized priesthood and the construction of the Tabernacle according to the pattern given to Moses on the mountain. The motifs related to this at *Ascension* are housebuilding, gold and silver temple vessels, and enthronement.

Testing

Here you will find references to the sun, moon and stars as heavenly or earthly rulers. It is also the place of corrupted rulers who are snakes, beasts and dragons. In the Garden, Satan as corrupted ruler tested Adam and usurped the authority Adam would have received if he had been faithful.

The seven lights of the Lampstand are also the

"governing" eyes of the Lord, so there is often a reference to eyes, to sight, or ironically to blindness. As a "garden of Satan," this central point concerns testing in the wilderness.

Maturity

This concerns the Covenant "body." It is fundamentally "plural." It concerns armies, or "hosts." The symbols all picture multitudes, so some unlikely companions are tied together here: birds and fish, incense clouds, brothers, soldiers, and cold, hard cash.

This step fills the firmament formed on Day 2, so the concept behind all of these symbols is an abundance of plunder filling the Tabernacle.

It is also the forming of an "Eve" body for the Adam "head." Adam is singular, but Eve, the mother of all living, is plural. *Maturity* is a cloud ascending to God, a shining entity that acts as one, a "collective noun" unified by the Spirit under the Covenant head and reflecting His glory.

Here there are also references to Moses repeating the Law to the next generation, which matches *Ascension* in the chiasm: the *Bronze* Altar matches the *Incense* Altar. The Bronze Altar warrior-priests are purified by *Testing* and transformed into Incense Altar elder-priests. Both have aromas that please God. The Bronze Altar aroma comes from death—roasting meat (Adam) and the Incense Altar is the fragrant, plural, resurrection of Eve.

Conquest

Besides the obvious symbols of conquest, here there are

references to Adam's High Priesthood: he carries the Covenant people from *Maturity* into *Glorification* as precious gems on his bosom, via the opened veil through which the High Priest would pass once a year.

Perhaps the most interesting factor is the frequent play on the two identical goats on the Day of Atonement. The concept of this final "body" *Division* is extremely serious, obvious in Jesus' separation of the sheep and goats.

This brings us to the most important symbol of *Conquest:* the Laver. Mirroring the Red Sea at *Division,* water is a recurring motif here, in everything from the Jordan River to New Covenant baptism. It is the ascension of the saints to stand on the crystal sea before God's throne and govern as a corporate mediator.

Glorification

This final step not only brings the cycle to an end but sets up the next one. It enthrones the completed church, head and body (captain and army), as a corporate mediator for the nations.

As Tabernacles, here you will find vines and fig trees, wine and oil. It is an "ingathering" and a great feast. This new marriage of heaven and earth produces godly offspring. They are commissioned and sent out to dominate the world as new *Creation*-words. They are pictured as children, letters, rivers, or even swift horses.

Glorification is both a rest for the faithful parents/ conquerors/overcomers of the old cycle, and a new Light that initiates a greater *Creation* week.

We'll give this a practice run with Exodus 17 and Daniel 1, and then begin with Adam's *Testing* in the Garden.

COMMENTS

This is an easy one.

Moses speaks the initiating "word" as the mediator under God.

Joshua obeys and makes an "exodus."

Moses "ascends" with the priest and the "king" (Hur was a leader from Judah).

Amalek, the perpetual enemy of God's people, is the embodiment of the serpent.

Moses is enthroned among the elders, united with his government as military commander over the troops.

The blood on the **Day of Atonement** was presented for all Israel in the dark. Here, Israel is freed from Amalek in the dark.

The celebration and sacrifice have a "marriage" theme. Israel is a corporate "warrior bride."

Creation - Moses commands Joshua to fight with Amalek

    Division - Joshua obeys and goes out to fight

        Ascension - Moses, Aaron and Hur ascend the mountain

            Testing - When Moses holds up his staff as mediator, Joshua prevails. When he tires, Amalek prevails

            Maturity - Moses sits on a stone, and Aaron and Hur support his arms until it is dark

        Conquest - Joshua defeats Amalek with the edge of the sword

Glorification - Moses builds an altar called "The Lord is my Banner"

COMMENTS

As we are about to deal with Adam's failure, this passage, Daniel 1, shows us what happens when God's man refuses to seize the kingdom.

The Ark is missing, so the remaining Temple vessels here are the glory of the Lord going before His people.

The young men make an "exodus" as captives.

As wise-men-in-training, they "ascend" and stand (symbolically) at the right hand of the power. Notice the king's food and wine corresponds to grain and fruit. But grain and fruit are only a promise of kingdom. It seems Daniel recognized that these were kingdom symbols and refused to take them.

Unlike Adam, the faithful men obey God and eat only from the "tree of life." Here, it is literally "seeds," which reminds us of the food in the Garden. The Lampstand, the kingdom/wisdom tree, is given to them. They become the "governing lights."

Adam had to cover himself with leaves, but here the king showers them with gifts, including robes.

The young Judahites rule over the other wise men.

Finally, notice that the themes at each step are also chiastic, beginning with captivity. The chiasm is completed with a reference to the end of captivity, which Daniel lived to see. It moves from an Israel that was judged as Egypt to a resurrected Israel back in Canaan.

Daniel's death was also his **Booths** "ingathering" to be with his fathers, the time when he passed things on to the next generation for a new cycle.

Creation - Captivity: The glory of the Lord goes before His people as the articles from the Temple are taken to the treasure house of Nebuchadnezzar

Division - Priests: The young Judahites are taken to Babylon to be trained as Babylonian "court magicians"

Ascension - Gifts: As high priest of Babylon, Nebuchadnezzar appoints three years of training, with the king's food and wine

Testing - Miracle: Daniel and his friends refuse the food of "Egypt" and are fed miraculously by God in the wilderness. They are given new names

Maturity - Gifts: God gives them gifts of wisdom, interpretation, strength and beauty

Conquest - Priests: They are chosen to serve before the king, above all the other wise men

Glorification - Captivity: Daniel's ministry continues until the first year of the next empire, the proclamation that brings the end of the seventy year captivity

COMMENTS

Finally, if my premise is to hold your attention, I think I should show how the entire Bible follows the pattern.

This chart will make more sense later on. It appears again at the end of the book, and we will be checking off each step as we get to it in our overview of Bible history. Based on what we cover along the way, I hope it demonstrates how important this study of "systematic typology" can be in our understanding of Bible history and Bible prophecy.

Then, we begin at the beginning...

ARK
Creation - World united as one blood   *(Sabbath)*
NOAH

VEIL
Division - World divided by blood   *(Passover)*
ABRAHAM - CIRCUMCISION - HEAD

BRONZE ALTAR
Ascension - Centralized priesthood   *(Firstfruits)*
ISRAEL - EARTHLY MEDIATORS

LAMPSTAND
Testing - The harvest begins   *(Pentecost)*
THE CHRIST

INCENSE ALTAR
Maturity - Centralized priesthood   *(Trumpets)*
FIRSTFRUITS CHURCH -
HEAVENLY MEDIATORS

LAVER
Conquest - World divided by water *(Atonement)*
THE WHOLE CHRIST - BAPTISM - BODY

REST
Glorification - World united by one Spirit *(Booths)*
ETERNITY

7

ADAM

YOU'VE DONE WELL TO GET THIS FAR, and I've got good news: *we've now covered the basics* and can get right into seeing how the Bible uses them. The first two major cycles, Adam and the flood, are important foundations for the rest of the Bible. You might want to keep a Bible handy from now on.

A crucial element to grasp here is that of "head and body." Adam goes through the pattern as the head of the human race. Then the race itself goes through the pattern. Adam *builds* the house and Eve *fills* it. Adam is structure; Eve is glory.

We will see this again in Moses and the Hebrews, in Jesus and the first century church, and in Israel and the nations. As with a human birth, God's design is always *head first*.

"For everyone who has will be given more,
and he will have an abundance.
Whoever does not have,
even what he has will be taken from him.
And throw that worthless servant outside,
into the darkness,
where there will be weeping
and gnashing of teeth."

(MATTHEW 25:29-30)

COMMENTS

Adam and Eve were naked because they were like children. This first cycle was designed by God to bring them to the first step of maturity. But Adam sold his birthright for food and an immediate kingdom.

Notice that the "door" to the Garden later became the veil in the Tabernacle, and the guarding cherubim became the Levite priests.

Here, Adam failed as High Priest. From now on, a blood sacrifice was required for man to approach God.

Adam corrupted the pattern by failing the test. He was unfaithful in little, and could be given no greater priestly responsibility.

- **Creation** - Adam is anointed to reflect the image of God, and he is given the Word, a single law

  - **Division** - Adam is divided, and his counterpart, Eve, is built

    - **Ascension** - They are united by covenant (nearbringing) when the Lord marries them

      - **Testing** - Adam's priesthood is tested. Would he open God's Law to fill Eve with light? Would he keep the sanctuary pure and qualify to expand his dominion to the outlying lands?

      - **Maturity** - Adam seizes dominion, rather than receiving it after obedience as a gift. They cover themselves with fig leaves

  - **Conquest** - But God uncovers the sin. Adam blames the Lord and Eve for his disobedient mismanagement. Adam and Eve have imaged the beast, rather than imaging God. Animal blood covers their sin. Animal skins cover their nakedness. They are on the wrong end of the *Conquest* sword. With blood shed at the Garden door, Adam is driven through the "veil" and enters the "Promised Land" without God. Fellowship without a covering (sacrifice) is denied

- **Glorification** - Adam's cursed dominion is multiplied in his offspring. He is banned from the mountain of God

COMMENTS

Using our "systematic typology" to correspond Adam's "body" pattern with that of Moses, we can see that Adam as "head" was like a failed Joshua.

At *Maturity*, he was still immature. His conquest was actually defeat, and his glory, his "army" or offspring (a frequent Bible picture), was corrupted. We see the consequences in the next cycle, the next generation.

Notice that the Lord calls Cain to be a "ruling light" Lampstand, the Law in human flesh, but instead he follows the serpent.

Cain is "marked" at **Atonement**. Here, the Lord is the High Priest. It seems that Cain despises God's mercy and becomes the second goat carrying the sins into the wilderness.

The witnesses against Cain appear at *Maturity*. Watch out for this later on.

You can see that the basic themes of the first seven books of the Bible align with this cycle very well. Cain's failure to judge rightly as a ruler corresponds with both Adam's failure and also the failure of Israel in the book of Judges.

Creation - Adam knows his wife and she bears the first son of man *(Sabbath)*

Division - She also bears Abel, who is a keeper of sheep. Cain works the ground *(Passover)*

Ascension - At the prescribed time, the brothers present offerings at the Garden door. Cain brings vegetables, but Abel brings the firstborn of his flock, and the fat portions. The Lord rejects Cain's offering and he is angry *(Firstfruits)*

Testing - The Lord warns him that sin is crouching at the door to the Garden (before the Throne), but that he must rule over it *(Pentecost)*

Maturity - Cain calls his brother into the field, rises up against him and slays him. When the Lord asks where Abel is, Cain replies, "Am I my brother's keeper?" Abel's blood cries to God from the ground. There are two witnesses: the Land and the blood *(Trumpets)*

Conquest - In God's mercy, Cain is marked. He goes "away from the presence of the Lord," cursed with barrenness *(Atonement)*

Glorification - In the land of wandering, he builds a counterfeit city to survive. As Adam resorted to cover himself on the "Day of the Lord," this city is Cain's "fig leaf" glory *(Booths)*

Eve was to be Adam's glory. Cain's city was his glory. This correspondence between the bride and the city can be traced right through the Bible. Peter Leithart writes:

> "Even before Cain, there is a hint—only a hint, but a hint—of a better city to come. It is not good for man to be alone, Yahweh says of Adam, and then takes a rib from Adam's side and makes that rib into a woman.

> Eve is not a city. But Eve is the prototype of a different sort of city, a bridal city. The hint is in the strange verb that Genesis 2:22 uses. Yahweh doesn't make or form Eve from the rib of Adam, but 'builds' the woman. Eve is the first thing built in the Bible, and the second thing to be built is Cain's city—that's the next use of that verb.

> But it's not just the verb that links the two. Cain builds his city after killing his brother, shedding Abel's blood on the ground. Adam goes into deep sleep, not death, and his flesh is opened up. The first time flesh is opened is not with Abel but with Adam. There is no reference to blood, but there must have been.

> There are key differences that highlight the differences of two cities. Cain kills his brother and founds his city on the blood of his brother; Adam's bride is built from his own body, from a kind of self-sacrifice. Further, Cain built his city; but Adam's bride is built by God. Eve is not a city,

but she is the prototype of the city that Abraham looked forward to, the city whose builder and maker is God.

The clearest evidence for this civic interpretation of the creation of Eve comes from the end of the Bible, where the city-bride is revealed in a thoroughly Edenic passage. The city-bride is a new Eve, adorned for her Husband, the Lamb, and this means that the original creation of Eve anticipated the consummation."[1]

---

1 Peter J. Leithart, *Bridal City,* www.leithart.com

COMMENTS

As head, Adam corrupted Eve by not stepping in when she was deceived. He corrupted his children by allowing sin and death into the world. And of course, he corrupted the human race, which eventually brought a judgment of total destruction in a global flood.

Due to Adam, all three domains, Garden, Land and World, were corrupted. Man had now sinned against Father, Son and Spirit.

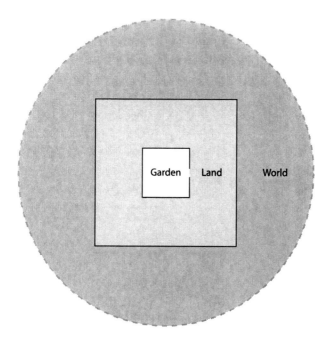

COMMENTS

Even though it involves Noah, this is Adam's "body" cycle, the army, which I call the "Greater Eve." In this cycle the flood is the Laver at *Conquest.* Noah will have his own cycle as "head," in which the flood is the waters parted at *Division.*

Notice the chiastic correspondence between the Spirit and the dove, the preaching of Enoch and Noah, and the death of **Passover** and the resurrection of **Atonement**. And, as usual, the "snake" is in the centre at *Testing.*

Just as animals were substituted for Adam to pay for his sin, animals were also substituted for Adam's race in the ark.

Creation - The Spirit hovers over the deep. The Land appears out of the water. The animals are brought to Adam. Judgment comes to Adam after seven days. Animal substitutes are killed to cover his sin *(Sabbath)*

> **Division** - Abel is slain, and Cain's household journeys into the wilderness *(Passover)*

>> **Ascension** - Lamech usurps the role of Covenant head and founds a false priesthood and a false Tabernacle. Enosh is born to replace Abel, and men *draw near* to God. Seth and Enoch bring the LAW. Enoch ascends to God *(Firstfruits)*

>>> **Testing** - The woman's and serpent's offspring intermarry. The Sethite/Cainite divided kingdom is reunited but not according to the true Covenant. The resulting "mighty men" are evil. The Lord JUDGES them *(Pentecost)*

>> **Maturity** - Noah repeats the LAW. The ark is built as a replacement Tabernacle. The animals are summoned to Noah as a replacement "body" *(Trumpets)*

> **Conquest** - Noah's family is "resurrected" behind the door. Sinners are condemned *(Atonement)*

Glorification - Judgment comes after seven days. The Land disappears under water. The dove hovers over the deep, and the ark *rests* on a new mountain *(Booths)*

8

TWO DOORS

IN THE DOMINION PATTERN THERE ARE TWO DOORS. The first is **Passover** *(Division),* when the Lord covers His people and draws them from the world to Himself in the wilderness to be tested. The second door is **Atonement** *(Conquest),* when the Lord assembles His trained people as a holy army to conquer a new world. Both doors involve water and blood. We see this pattern again at the exodus. **Passover** preceded the Red Sea, and bloody **Jericho** followed the Jordan.

The floating basket that Jochebed used to save her baby, Moses, was a self-contained *doorway.* It was waterproofed with a *covering* (pitch), the same word used of the covering on Noah's ark. Like Noah, Moses was God's mediator, or *door,* in a box sealed, or *covered,* for protection.

The doors of the Hebrew homes in Goshen were also *"covered"* (with blood) for protection from the Avenging Angel.

God later commanded Moses to have the Ark constructed to carry His Ten Words, the commandments. Once a year, on the Day of Atonement (Coverings), the High Priest could safely pass through the veil, standing at the *doorway* to heaven as the representative of the Land. He sprinkled blood before the Ark seven times for the sins of the people, as a covering for Adam's corrupted week.

Finally, in Christ, we have the Word in human flesh, an open *doorway* who protected the faithful once and for all with the "covering" of His blood.

The Dominion pattern can be distilled to a basic "progressive" chiasm. It will make more sense later on, but for now, notice the two doors. The first concerns the covering of the head (Adam), and the second concerns the covering of the body (Eve).

Sabbath - initiating Word

Passover - blood and water
(**Red Sea - death**)

Firstfruits - presentation of head

Pentecost - **head rules body**

Trumpets - presentation of body

Atonement - water and blood
(**Jordan - resurrection**)

Booths - head and body united in God

PRIEST - HEAD

Creation - King Adam

Division
exit: people purified by blood and water

Ascension - Adam ascends as family head

Testing - Opportunity for growth and wisdom

Maturity - Eve expands the family to a holy army

Conquest - **entry: land purified by water and blood**

Glorification - City Eve

PEOPLE - BODY

FORMING
(Adam)
CAPTAIN - LIGHT

FILLING
(Eve)
ARMY - LIGHTS

9

NOAH

NOAH MEANS "REST." As the Sabbath-king of Adam's "body" pattern, Noah was given a glorious robe, and power as a judge to sentence murderers to death. Noah was like the first King Solomon. Solomon, like *shalom,* means "Peace."

Noah's "head" pattern leads to more success than Adam's did. After the flood, God commanded Noah's line to have children and fill the *World.* He gave Noah the authority to execute murderers, like Cain, in the *Land.* And Noah planted a *Garden*—a vineyard.

Garden corrupted

Land corrupted

World corrupted

World destroyed by God

World new dominion

Land new law

Garden new keeper

COMMENTS

Ham became the serpent in Noah's garden. Noah's robe symbolized his new government. Like Adam, Ham tried to seize the kingdom without first being proven as an obedient servant.

Creation - Call of Noah *(Sabbath)*

Division - Noah's exodus through the flood *(Passover)*

Ascension - God's blessing. Noah makes a sacrifice (a "near-bringing") *(Firstfruits)*

Testing - Ham seizes the robe of rulership, uncovers nakedness and disgraces his father *(Pentecost)*

Maturity - Two witnesses: Noah's other two sons restore the robe. The sons are assembled before him *(Trumpets)*

Conquest - Noah judges between his sons. He blesses his obedient sons and curses Ham for his sin *(Atonement)*

Glorification - The sons of Noah multiply into seventy nations *(Booths)*

However, Noah's Land cycle still ended with a "city of Cain." Nimrod (Gilgamesh) was not a wise judge. He was not a shepherd but a wild beast, a hunter. He considered himself "the mighty vanquisher of God,"[1] and his city-temple-tower was built on a crooked foundation. It was a false Tabernacle. Nimrod means "Rebel."

Instead of expanding the kingdom and achieving glory for God, the people wanted a name (glory) for themselves.

The Joktanites were children of Shem. Instead of remaining separate from the rebel kingdom, they compromised with the offspring of the serpent.

The tower to heaven was a shortcut to glory, a self-serving *Glorification*. It fell so short that the Lord had to "come down" to "measure" the temple of this wild beast.

---

1 See *Who was Nimrod?* by Bible archaeologist
   Dr. David P. Livingston, www.biblearchaeology.org

 COMMENTS

Notice that the Lord comes down at **Pentecost** but finds disobedience. Instead of unity at **Trumpets**, there is scattering.

The reference to the Gate of God aligns with the High Priest on the **Day of Atonement**, standing at the veil.

Booths was also known as "Ingathering." The opposite happens at the end of this cycle.

Creation - The resting world has one language *(Sabbath)*

Division - The sons of Shem journey from the east *(Passover)*

Ascension - They decide to build a tower to heaven, a false Tabernacle *(Firstfruits)*

Testing - The Lord comes down to assess them *(Pentecost)*

Maturity - Two witnesses: God (as plural) witnesses the disobedience and decides to confuse their language, scattering them across the Land *(Trumpets)*

Conquest - The site is named Babel, which means "Gate of God" *(Atonement)*

Glorification - The world is divided when God confuses language and religion, scattering the "children" across the Land *(Booths)*

Adam disobeyed God in the *Garden* and was cast out.
Cain killed his brother in the *Land* and was cast out.
The sons of God married unbelievers in the *World* and
were cast out. In these three domains, man sinned
against Father, Son and Spirit. James Jordan writes:

> "Man's first fall, in the Sanctuary, prevented his
> going into Eden and resulted in his being put in a
> Homeland that was not a Throneland. The
> second fall, of Cain, expelled him from a
> Homeland into a world of wandering. The third
> fall, of the Sethites, removed the sinners from the
> world through the great flood.
>
> ...these rebellions constituted stealing the gift of
> the Father (sacrilege), murder of the brotherhood
> of the Son (fratricide), and resisting the marital
> gifts of the Spirit (intermarriage or compro-
> mise)."[2]

Like Adam, Ham seized the robe of authority in the
Garden. Nimrod built a "city of Cain" in the *Land.* But
there is no *World* cycle. James Jordan writes:

> "We don't directly see the sin of Fratricide here,
> but the other parallels link it to Cain's fall in the
> land. Cain was cursed to wander, though he did
> build a city. The story of the Tower and City of
> Babel shows judgment of scattering, analogous to
> the judgment of Cain... we don't have a third

2 James B. Jordan, *The Production of the New Testament Canon:
A Revisionist Suggestion,* BIBLICAL HORIZONS No. 56,
www.biblicalhorizons.com

rebellion in the world-setting, because God does not intend to destroy the world again. Instead, we have three positive pictures presented in the next spiral."[3]

Joseph, Abraham's faithful great-grandson, ruled the world.

Adam - Garden

Noah - Garden, Land

Abraham - Garden, Land, World

3 James B. Jordan, *Through New Eyes,* Volume II, BIBLICAL HORIZONS No. 57, www.biblicalhorizons.com

10

ABRAHAM

ADAM'S FAILURE BROUGHT **physical** *De-Creation.* Cain founded a corrupt civilization whose evil influence triumphed. Just like Cain, Ham was cursed, and his son Canaan's influence led to **social** *De-Creation.*

As God raised new land out of the waters after the flood, God would now perform a similar *Re-Creation* miracle. In calling Abram, God was socially dividing the waters of the nations into the Land and the Sea.

Creation - A world united as one blood *(Sabbath)*

Division - A world divided by blood *(Passover)*

In this way, human history moved from *Creation* to *Division.* The era of the patriarchs, ruling fathers, began. God called Abram and tore "Adam" in two. It was the initiation by God of the Jew-Gentile divide. Peter Leithart writes:

> "In Genesis 9:11, Yahweh promises not to "cut off flesh" by water. That is the covenant with Noah. A few chapters later, Yahweh tells Abram that he must cut off the flesh of all male children of Israel, not by water but by a knife."[1]

---

1   Peter J. Leithart, *Cutting Off Flesh,* www.leithart.com

As a new, more faithful Adam, the Lord would test Abram in Garden, Land and World.

 COMMENTS

At *Division*, the sons of Shem moved *east* and ended up in sin. At *Division*, Abram moved *west* to Canaan.

The serpent was still behind the scenes, trying to thwart God's promise of the woman's offspring who would crush his head (Genesis 3:15). In both Pharaoh's and Abimelech's attempts to seize the bride from her lord, the serpent's attack on Eve was repeated.

ABRAM'S GARDEN

Creation - God calls Abram *(Sabbath)*

Division - Terah dies. Abram removes himself from death in the east (Babylon [Shinar]) to life in Canaan *(Passover)*

Ascension - Abram builds an altar at Shechem (at an oak tree) and at Bethel *(Firstfruits)*

Testing - Famine in Canaan: Abram as priest fails to ask the Lord for food (Tree of Life) and relocates to Egypt. The Lord protects Sarai from Pharaoh (the serpent) and Abram departs *(Pentecost)*

Maturity - God warns Pharaoh's house with horrible plagues but blesses Abram with servants and animals *(Trumpets)*

Conquest - With the plunder, Abram has extended the house of God and returns to Bethel *(Atonement)*

Glorification - Instead of dominating the land with Abram, Lot leaves the Garden of God. He moves east to a counterfeit garden, as his ancestors did—the city of Sodom *(Booths)*

COMMENTS

Abram's Garden-worship led to dominion over the Land. He refused the plunder of this holy war and was entertained as a king by the Lord's priest. And he rescued Lot as well.

ABRAM'S LAND

Creation - God's Word to Abram promises the four corners of the Land. His offspring will be "dust"—a new Adam *(Sabbath)*

> **Division** - Abram moves away from Lot to Hebron *(Passover)*

> > **Ascension** - He builds an altar in a garden of oak trees *(Firstfruits)*

> > > **Testing** - The serpent gathers a conspiracy of nations, who carry away captive the local rulers *(Pentecost)*

> > **Maturity** - Abram shows courage and local authority by defeating these usurping kings with the men of his house *(Trumpets)*

> **Conquest** - The righteous are separated from the wicked, the enemies are plundered and the land is freed *(Atonement)*

Glorification - The Gentile priest/king Melchizedek brings bread and wine. He blesses Abram as a king *(Booths)*

COMMENTS

This next cycle is actually only the first step of Abram's World. Seven cycles make up the complete cycle.

During Abram's deep sleep, he is "passed *over*." At **Atonement**, the sacrifices are the veil passed *through*.

Passover was only for the mediator-nation. But **Booths** was a feast that Gentiles were invited to attend. We see this reflected here.

Creation - The Lord calls Abram outside. He shows him the stars, and Abram receives the Word with faith *(Sabbath)*

Division - Abram divides the animals, chases away the birds of prey and falls into a deep sleep at sunset *(Passover)*

Ascension - Abram receives the "pattern" from God concerning his descendants *(Firstfruits)*

Testing - They will be slaves in Egypt for 400 years *(Pentecost)*

Maturity - The Lord will judge their oppressors and bring them out with great plunder *(Trumpets)*

Conquest - In the darkness, a smoking firepot (body) and blazing torch (head) pass through the divided pieces *(Atonement)*

Glorification - The Land is given to Abram's offspring and its borders are measured among the Gentiles *(Booths)*

COMMENTS

As mentioned earlier, the Tabernacle was an image of the Creation. In Exodus 25-31, there are seven speeches given by God to Moses concerning its construction. The instructions put the Tabernacle elements in the order of the Creation Week. This begins to come to prominence in this cycle. Notice that the Bronze Altar *(Ascension)* and the Incense Altar *(Maturity)* are matched in the symmetry.

Lot sat in the gate of Sodom as a judge, a governing light. He was grieved by the citizens' sins but no doubt forced to compromise. At the *Testing* in this cycle, he is dethroned by the uncompromising Law of God.

At *Conquest* in this cycle, it is Abraham, not God, doing the "passing through."

ABRAM'S WORLD

Creation - Covenant Promise: God hovers over the "Abyss" and makes a "new Land" by purifying Abram's Garden with blood (Ark) *(Sabbath)*

   Division - Disobedience: Abram and Sarah seize the glory of offspring prematurely through the Egyptian slave. Abram mediates for Ishmael and God blesses Ishmael's offspring (Veil) *(Passover)*

   Ascension - Priesthood: Abram circumcises his offspring, and his family becomes a living sacrifice for the nations. Sarah conceives Isaac (Altar and Table) *(Firstfruits)*

   Testing - Judgment: Lot is dethroned. Sodom and Gomorrah are destroyed by fire from heaven (Lampstand) *(Pentecost)*

   Maturity - Witness: Abraham deals wisely with Abimelech (Incense) *(Trumpets)*

Conquest - Coverings: Abraham enters the Promised Land to sacrifice Isaac. He enters again to buy a cave for Sarah's burial (Laver/High Priest) *(Atonement)* [2]

Glorification - Covenant Succession: Rebekah (Shekinah) *(Booths)*

---

2 On the Day of Atonement (Coverings), the High Priest approached the Most Holy Place twice: once for the priesthood and once for the people. We see this reflected here. Isaac is the covered priesthood; Sarah is the covered people.

COMMENTS

Here is the outline of the first **Atonement** cycle.

In cycle five's *Conquest,* Abraham gave seven ewes to Abimelech to remain in peace in his land. Here, he returned to the same site, the "well of seven."

Both these steps correspond to the High Priest sprinkling blood seven times towards the Ark in the Most Holy Place on the Day of Atonement (the Laver).

Creation - The Lord asks Abraham to sacrifice his "only son" *(Sabbath)*

 Division - Abraham briefly enters the Promised Land *(Passover)*

  Ascension - Abraham directs Isaac to God as provider and builds the altar for the sacrifice *(Firstfruits)*

   Testing - Abraham binds Isaac and takes the knife *(Pentecost)*

  Maturity - Isaac is presented to God as the next generation. The Lord speaks again to Abraham, stopping him *(Trumpets)*

 Conquest - The ram is substituted for Isaac as the ascension, and God promises a greater house. Abraham returns to Beersheba (well of seven) *(Atonement)*

Glorification - Abraham's brother Nahor has eight children, and one of them (Bethuel) is father to Rebekah (a new bride) *(Booths)*

COMMENTS

Concerning the promised offspring, Abraham's entire narrative follows the pattern.

The bread and wine of Melchizedek's *Glorification* of Abraham now appear as **Firstfruits**, the grain and fruit plants of Day 3.

The Covenant-makings at **Firstfruits** and **Trumpets** are chiastic. The first corresponds to Moses *receiving* the Law on Sinai as Covenant "head." The second is Moses *repeating* the Law to the Covenant "body" in Deuteronomy.

The Lord's Lampstand eyes "oversee" Hagar and Ishmael at the centre, which suggests that Abraham's mediation for Gentiles was the centre of God's purpose for Israel.

THE DOMINION OF ABRAHAM

Creation - Abram is called to leave Ur
(*Sabbath*)

    Division - Sarai is protected from Pharaoh.
Lot departs (*Passover*)

        Ascension - Abram "ascends" as a king
and is blessed by Melchizedek (bread
and wine). The Lord makes a Covenant
with him (*Firstfruits*)

            Testing - Abraham conceives with
Hagar. Hagar is thrown out but given
water in the wilderness. She calls the
Lord "You-Are-the-God-Who-Sees."
Ishmael is born (*Pentecost*)

        Maturity - The Lord makes a Covenant
with him. Abraham oversees the land.
Isaac is born (*Trumpets*)

    Conquest - Abraham enters the Land to
offer Isaac. Isaac is spared, and the ram is
sacrificed (*Atonement*)

Glorification - Sarah dies. Both Abraham
and Isaac find wives. Abraham has six more
sons by Keturah. Isaac succeeds Abraham
(*Booths*)

"Well done, good and faithful servant.
You have been faithful over a little;
I will set you over much.
Enter into the joy of your master."

(MATTHEW 25:21)

11

JACOB

ANCIENT MAN WANTED TO BUILD HIS WAY BACK UP TO GOD. There are still pyramids and ziggurats to remind us of his preoccupation with a garden on a mountain, and access to heaven requiring blood sacrifice. Eden is not one of the legends; it is their historical source.

Eden, with its Garden, was situated on a mountain or plateau. We know this because four rivers flowed out of it, and rivers only flow downstream. Imagine a mountain with four sides, its top shrouded in cloud. God's throne in heaven is higher than the firmament, so the actual mountaintop is higher than the Garden, where man rules under God. God comes down in a fiery cloud to bring man His Word and assess his works. The cloud is His chariot. Without the fall, men would have followed the rivers to the ends of the earth, carrying God's Spirit within them as miniature temples. Like the stars moving across the sky, this holy army in glorious robes would fill the world.

After Adam and Eve sinned and were expelled from the Garden, man was still to come before God with sacrifices at the end of harvest. Not only was there holy fire at the door of the Garden to keep man out, the beast was still before the door, acting as an accuser before the throne of the Judge. When God warned Cain that sin was lying at the door, seeking to devour him, it was more than just a metaphor. Judgment begins at the house of God, but so does temptation. The serpent was still in the Garden of God, standing between man and glory as both tempter and counsel for the prosecution.

Cain and Abel understood that the death of the beast opened the door to fellowship with God. Abel's sins were covered by his offering of a sheep. But Cain's vegetables, the work of his hands, were like the leaves Adam and Eve used to cover their own nakedness. Only blood can atone for—*cover*—sin.

After Cain murdered his brother, the Land vomited him out. No garden, no vegetables. Cain's impatient reach for a robe of glory was to build a city (Enoch) to cover himself. He manufactured a mountain of God, founded on the blood of his brother.

The children of Joktan (Shemites) *compromised* to build their own mountain in the east (the direction of exile), the city and tower of Babel. This was their impatient grab at glory. But God started from scratch with a new garden in Abraham. Because His people do not resort to robbery and exploitation, God's cities take time to build.

The promise of Canaan to Abraham's children would put the Shemites back at the centre of the world. The Hebrews would be surrounded by Canaanites. Like the serpent, the Lord would use the Canaanites to test His people.

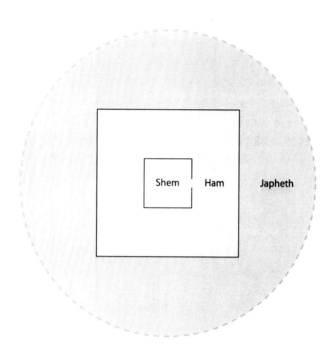

After Noah's new Garden, Babel was the tower in the "Land." In Abraham's new Garden, Isaac's failure to judge rightly (symbolized by his blindness) meant that Jacob replaced him. It was to Jacob that the Lord showed His blueprint for a true Babel in the Land, a tower to heaven, a new "mountain of God."

With his head on a rough stone, Jacob saw angels ascending and descending on a stairway to heaven, a spiritual ziggurat between God and man. Symbolically, Jacob was on the Bronze Altar, looking up through the heavenly Tabernacle towards the Most Holy Place.

God wouldn't build this tower out of bricks and mortar, however; as with Eve, He would build it out of flesh and blood—Jacob's offspring—a living Temple, made of precious stones mined from the Land.

COMMENTS

This cycle covers the entire Jacob narrative but there are also cycles within it. See if you can find these yourself.

THE DOMINION OF JACOB

Creation - Jacob receives the Covenant blessing from Isaac *(Sabbath)*

Division - Esau is rejected. Jacob flees *(Passover)*

Ascension - In a dream, with his head on an "altar," he sees the pattern of the heavenly Tabernacle *(Firstfruits)*

Testing - Jacob is tested by Laban *(Pentecost)*

Maturity - Jacob fights with the angel of the Lord and receives the blessing (plunder). He is given a new name—"Israel." Jacob is reconciled with his brother *(Trumpets)*

Conquest - There is war with the Shechemites. The false gods are buried (covered/entombed) *(Atonement)*

Glorification - Rachel dies bearing Jacob's twelfth son. Jacob succeeds Isaac *(Booths)*

12

JOSEPH

Unlike Adam, Abraham was a faithful priest in the *Garden,* obediently offering Isaac. Unlike Cain, Jacob made peace with his brother and his uncle in the *Land.* Joseph would be tested like his fathers. Unlike the sons of God, he would resist the "daughters of men" (Potiphar's wife) and dominate the Canaanite *World.*

Abraham - Garden

Jacob - Land

Joseph - World

The narrative of Joseph's life itself follows the Garden, Land, World pattern.

COMMENTS

The importance of Joseph's robe of office is chiastic. At **Passover**, he is the Temple veil, and at **Atonement** he is the torn veil.

Joseph has two dreams—two witnesses from the Lord. Notice also that Joseph becomes the second "witness" as a potential martyr at *Maturity*.

Joseph is a single mediator at *Creation*, and at *Glorification* he is sent to become a "corporate" mediator, establishing a greater house for Jacob.

JOSEPH'S GARDEN

Creation - Joseph speaks to his father against the crimes of his brothers *(Sabbath)*

Division - Joseph is **covered** with a robe, and his brothers hate him *(Passover)*

Ascension - Joseph has a "harvest" dream of his dominion over his brothers *(Firstfruits)*

Testing - His second dream concerns his rulership over the Sun, Moon and Stars *(Pentecost)*

Maturity - An angel "witness" "presents" the brothers to Joseph. His brothers seize him and threaten to kill him *(Trumpets)*

Conquest - Reuben mediates for Joseph, who is thrown into a pit. Joseph's robe is **covered** with the blood of a goat as a substitute *(Atonement)*

Glorification - Jacob thinks his favorite son has been torn to pieces, but Joseph is carried to Egypt *(Booths)*

COMMENTS

In the Garden cycle, Joseph was a faithful prophet. Now he was a faithful priest to Potiphar. In his World cycle, he was a faithful king. Joseph's life embodied—incarnated—Word, Sacrament and Government.

JOSEPH'S LAND

Creation - Dominion is stolen from Joseph the prophet. Joseph is drawn from the pit *(Sabbath)*

Division - Joseph's "death" is faked, and he is left "naked" after his glorious robe is taken from him. He is transported to Egypt *(Passover)*

Ascension - Joseph ascends to serve Potiphar and is given **authority** over his house. All Potiphar has to worry about is his bread *(Firstfruits)*

Testing - Like the "daughters of men," Potiphar's wife attempts to seduce Joseph *(Pentecost)*

Maturity - He resists her advances, but again loses his robe of **authority** *(Trumpets)*

Conquest - Joseph is thrown into prison *(Atonement)*

Glorification - As a faithful servant, he is again given authority over the "house" *(Booths)*

COMMENTS

It is interesting that the scavenging birds in the baker's dream appear at the same step in the pattern as the birds Abraham chased away. With Joseph behind the prison door, the bread is broken so the wine can be poured out.

It is important to note that at *Maturity*, Joseph marries a Gentile bride. This event corresponds to the animals submitting to Noah, and eventually to Gentiles joining the Christian church as "plunder" from the nations.

JOSEPH'S WORLD

Creation - As a faithful servant, Joseph is again given authority *(Sabbath)*

Division - Joseph predicts the death of Pharaoh's baker and the reinstatement of his **cup**bearer (bread and wine) *(Passover)*

Ascension - He is finally called up before Pharaoh to interpret the king's dreams *(Firstfruits)*

Testing - Joseph brings wise counsel from God to avoid a famine, becomes a "father" to Pharaoh, and is given a new robe and a throne *(Pentecost)*

Maturity - He marries a Gentile bride (plunder) and has children *(Trumpets)*

Conquest - Joseph tests his brothers concerning Benjamin and has them imprisoned for the theft of Pharaoh's **cup**. The old tent of Jacob is torn down and incorporated into Joseph's house in a conquered Gentile land *(Atonement)*

Glorification - He seats his brothers in their birth order and allows them to partake in his own "resurrection." They feast together in his new kingdom. He rules the nations as their provider, not as a tyrant *(Booths)*

COMMENTS

Standing at Pharaoh's "right hand," Joseph himself is the **Firstfruits** of a greater pattern. As bread and wine "lifted up," he opens the "mystery of God" and is in charge of both Pharaoh's grain and Pharaoh's cup, and his people enjoy life in the fertile Land of Goshen.

As elders, Moses and Aaron summon the plagues, the swarms of Day 5, as warnings to Pharaoh.

Under Joshua, Israel destroys the Canaanites, and the Lord raises up wise Judges to keep Israel in the Promised Land.

From Canaan-promised to Canaan-delivered, Israel as a nation is a new Creation Week.

For this pattern to work seamlessly, Israel's *first* generation in the wilderness should have entered Canaan.

THE DOMINION OF ISRAEL

CANAAN PROMISED

Creation - Abraham and Isaac *(Sabbath)*

Division - Jacob and Esau *(Passover)*

Ascension - Joseph *(Firstfruits)*

Testing - Slavery in Egypt *(Pentecost)*

Maturity - Moses and Aaron *(Trumpets)*

Conquest - Joshua *(Atonement)*

Glorification - The Judges *(Booths)*

CANAAN DELIVERED

MOSES

THE LORD'S PROMISE TO ABRAHAM included the revelation that his offspring would be slaves for four centuries. Joseph's dominion did result in great multiplication, and his people lived in Goshen, a very fertile part of Egypt. God heard His people's prayers for deliverance, but waited until the right time to send a saviour.

What made the time of Moses right? Firstly, the Hebrews had grown to the size of a nation and, in a sense, had been punished for selling Joseph into slavery.

Secondly, in Genesis 10, 70 nations are listed before the tower of Babel. In Jacob's family, God had planted the seed of 70 people in Egypt, and a new nation that would bless all nations was ready to flourish. At the Feast of Booths, Israel was to sacrifice seventy bulls for the Gentile nations, mediating for them as priests before God.

Thirdly, God had told Abraham that the people currently living in the Promised Land still had time to repent. They had only become worse, and now their time was up. Joshua's Israel—the next generation— would bring holy, judicial violence as destroying "angels" against the Canaanites and *their* next generation—their children. Their "cycle" was cut off.

The most obvious appearance of the Dominion

pattern is the exodus from Egypt and conquest of Canaan. But the pattern is also stamped into Moses' life. In his personal pattern, Moses leaves the Hebrews and passes through the Nile to the wilderness of Egypt. It ends with the Lord's glorious appearance at the Garden door, in the burning bush on a mountain.

COMMENTS

Moses' judicial execution of the Egyptian is often interpreted as a failure. However, Moses had the authority to pass judgment and execute the sentence, and he later became the judge of his people. "Moses was instructed in all the wisdom of the Egyptians, and he was mighty in his words and deeds" (Acts 7:22). However, he feared Pharaoh's unjust reaction to his just deed.

In every other instance, the shedding of innocent blood requires the blood of the murderer to be shed. However, in this case, it was the Hebrews' rejection of Moses as their judge that condemned *them* to 40 years' more slavery. Like those whose bodies fell in the wilderness, it was the next generation who would be delivered.

MOSES AS PRIEST

Creation - Moses is born *(Sabbath)*

Division - Moses crosses the waters of the Nile (death) covered in a basket *(Passover)*

Ascension - Moses is adopted by Pharaoh's house *(Firstfruits)*

Testing - Like Abraham, Moses rightly *judges* between the Egyptian and the Hebrew *(Pentecost)*

Maturity - Moses is rejected as judge by his Hebrew brothers *(Trumpets)*

Conquest - Moses is separated from Egypt and joins the house of Jethro, Gentile high priest of Midian *(Atonement)*

Glorification - Moses marries and has children. He meets the Lord on the mountain *(Booths)*

COMMENTS

This pattern explains the necessity of the Lord's attempt to kill Moses' firstborn son. Blood was presented and the Destroyer passed over.

At *Ascension*, Moses stands at the right hand of the world power, rightly claiming the Hebrew people for God as their mediator, their advocate.

The plagues upon Egypt here correspond to the swarms in the sky and sea of Day 5. The Lord doesn't need horses and chariots. He can call an army up from nothing.

This facet of *Maturity* also shows us that under the Covenant, the blessings for obedience and curses for disobedience—plunder and plagues—are multiplications—revelations—of what is in our hearts (Psalm 1:3-4; James 1:12-18).

Notice that in the greater pattern, Moses receives the Law on Sinai at *Ascension*. Here, the elders of Israel represent both Israel and the Gentiles at a "Feast of Booths" on the mountain.

MOSES AS KING

40 YEARS IN THE WILDERNESS

Creation - The Lord speaks His word to Moses from the burning bush *(Sabbath)*

> **Division** - On the way to Egypt, the Lord intends to kill Moses' *firstborn son,* but Zipporah circumcises him (death) *(Passover)*

> > **Ascension** - Moses is reunited with the Hebrews and "ascends" to Pharaoh's court. He "opens the Law" to Pharaoh and his "angels," the court magicians *(Firstfruits)*

> > > **Testing** - Moses again judges between the Egyptian and the Hebrew. Aaron turns his staff into a serpent and it devours Pharaoh's serpents *(Pentecost)*

> > **Maturity** - Moses repeats God's Word and brings warning plagues (swarms) which uncover Egypt's gods *(Trumpets)*

> **Conquest** - The Avenging Angel takes the *un*-covered firstborn. Pharaoh's slaughter of Hebrew infants is atoned for. Jacob's *family* is resurrected as a *nation* through the divided waters of the Red Sea *(Atonement)*

Glorification - The Lord prepares a table in the wilderness, and Moses and the elders climb the mountain of God to dine with Him *(Booths)*

40 YEARS IN THE WILDERNESS

COMMENTS

Interestingly, if we combine these two previous cycles into one, the Creation/Tabernacle pattern becomes prominent, with the burning bush at the centre as the golden Lampstand in the Holy Place.

We cover the Creation/Tabernacle in the next chapter.

MOSES AS HEAD OF
A NEW CREATION

Creation - Ark/Light:
Moses is rescued, trained and given authority
(Sabbath)

   Division - Veil/Firmament:
   Moses' exodus from Egypt (death)
   (Passover)

      **Ascension - Bronze Altar and Table of
      Facebread/Land & Sea and Grain &
      Fruit Plants:** Moses stays in the house of
      Jethro the High Priest *(Firstfruits)*

         Testing - Lampstand/Ruling Lights:
         The (seven) eyes of the Lord—
         the burning bush—have seen the
         suffering of His people *(Pentecost)*

      Maturity - Incense Altar/Swarms:
      Moses is finally accepted as mediator for
      the Hebrew people, to bring them
      before the Lord *(Trumpets)*

   Conquest - Laver/Priesthood:
   He brings the Day of the Lord to Egypt...
   (Atonement)

Glorification - Shekinah/Rest:
...and an end to Hebrew slavery
(Booths)

14

WORLD-
IN-A-BOX

THE CALL OF ABRAM moved human history from
Creation to *Division*. The call of Moses moved it from
Division (a separate people) to a centralized priest-
hood—*Ascension*.

Before this time, there were many godly priests,
such as Melchizedek and Jethro. But now Israel, as
mediator for the world, was the *head* of the nations.
This prefigured the ascension of *Christ* as firstfruits,
representing mankind before the Father with shed
blood. Israel sacrificed animals that were ceremonially
clean. Jesus, being sinless, presented His own blood.

- **Creation** - A world united as one blood *(Sabbath)*

- **Division** - A world divided by blood *(Passover)*

- **Ascension** - A centralized priesthood
  (Firstfruits)

When the Lord makes a new Covenant in the Bible, it
is spoken of as a New Creation. The instructions for
the Tabernacle (Exodus 25-31) are seven speeches
which follow the pattern of the Creation Week. The
Tabernacle was a miniature "clean" world, a *micro-
cosmos*. It was the DNA for a new Creation.

DAY 1
LIGHT - THE ARK

The Ark of the Covenant was the Lord's footstool below His invisible throne. Ancient kings were carried in litters by their slaves, and God's throne was carried (under a cover) by His people. The Ark was never to be carried on an animal or a cart. As with kings, being carried by men was a reminder of God's rulership over them.

Gold is solid light. As God created light on the first day, the Ark was covered in gold. The lid on the Ark was actually solid gold. There was no natural light in the Most Holy Place. The Ark was the light.

 COMMENTS

As *Creation*, the Ark is the creative Word that starts the *Creation* to *Glorification* process.

DAY 2
FIRMAMENT - THE VEILS

As God stretched out the heavens like a garment or a tent, the Tabernacle had curtains or veils embroidered with silver and gold. As the firmament is an opaque barrier between heaven and man, so a veil obscured the Most Holy Place from the priests, and another veil obscured the Holy Place from the courtyard.

As the firmament is where the sun, moon, planets and stars rule the sky, the Holy Place was where man ruled the world under God. God's "living room" was also a Garden below the glory-cloud, and here the priesthood served Him as Adam did.

COMMENTS

As Day 2, the Veil is the blood-covered door of **Passover**. The firmament is also referred to as a Covenant scroll. It is a symbolic barrier protecting man from being face to face with the Law of God. When the Covenant is broken, this scroll is rolled up and replaced with a new Covenant. The old Holy Place is destroyed and rebuilt.

127

DAY 3
LAND AND SEA
THE BRONZE ALTAR

As God raised the land out of the waters, the Altar was the holy Land, perfectly square with four mountain peaks. God's consuming fire descended on the mountain and communed with man in the Garden, halfway down, inside the Altar. The peaks were also four horns, which were daubed with the blood of the sacrifice to purify the Land before God could visit. Horns symbolize the power to execute judgment. Blood-covered horns showed justice was satisfied.

COMMENTS

When the Bible appears to speak of a "flat earth," it is actually referring to Israel as the four-cornered Bronze Altar, mediating between heaven and earth above the "waters" of the nations. Israel is "lifted up" as a holy priesthood.

GRAIN AND FRUIT
THE TABLE OF SHOWBREAD

On the Table in the Holy Place were twelve loaves of
bread and jugs of beer, and later, when they entered the
Promised Land, **wine**. Like the **manna** and the **grapes**
of Eshcol *(Ascension)*, they were a promise of rest and
rule with God. They were types of a future permanent
Sabbath as priests and kings *(Glorification)*.

Just as the marriage covenant of Adam and Eve at
Firstfruits was really the betrothal of their united
marriage to God at Booths, so this Day 3 Table of
Israel was a promise of future glory to the whole world
on Day 7. Human marriage is a picture of future glory.

 COMMENTS ✐

Bread always comes before wine. Bread symbolizes
faithful obedience (priesthood). Wine symbolizes the
resulting wisdom (kingdom).

Day 4
Sun, Moon and Planets
the Gold Lampstand

The seven lights are the sun, moon and five bright planets that rule the firmament. The Lampstand overlooked the Table of Showbread as the burning eyes of God watching over man and giving him light (Law) to judge between good and evil *(Testing)*. Made of solid gold and constructed to look like an almond tree, it was a burning bush. As gold is *solid* light, the pure beaten olive oil is *liquid* light. The Lampstand is God's people as wise rulers filled with Light *(Pentecost)*.

COMMENTS

In the book of Numbers, the tribes were numbered and arranged around the Tabernacle "throne" of God as twelve constellations. They were a starry host moving across the "dark sky" of the wilderness until the "Day of the Lord" came with *Glorification* in Canaan.

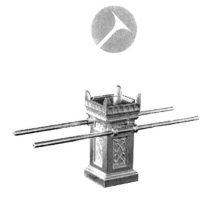

Day 5
Birds and Fish
the Incense Altar

"Swarms" of birds and fish filled what God divided on Day 2. The Incense Altar filled the Holy Place with clouds of perfumed smoke.

The birds symbolized the armies of heaven and the fish the armies of the nations.

 COMMENTS

This one is a bit weird, unless you are willing to think visually. Just as Moses was brought to God as "head," here the army is brought before God as "body." The clouds of incense symbolize the multitudes of God's government. At **Trumpets**, it is the troops of Israel. Sometimes it is angelic armies. In Revelation 4, it is the 24 elders with bowls of incense before the throne.

131

DAY 6
MEDIATOR
THE LAVER

Both the priests and the animals were washed in the Laver. The Tabernacle instructions position the Laver at Day 6—instead of with the "waters" of the Firmament—because Adam required resurrection to approach the Lord. This still matches Day 2 chiastically, as the Red Sea matches the Jordan.

ANIMALS AND MAN -
THE SACRIFICES AND THE PRIESTS

Clean animals were substituted as sacrifices to cover unclean men. Just as the priests were forbidden to wear shoes in God's house, so the clean animals included the ones careful about where they put their feet.

 COMMENTS

As the Jordan, the Laver corresponds to the crystal sea before the Throne of God. Clean feet walk on the Sea.

Day 7
Rest - Pillar of Fire

The Tabernacle was a symbolically sanitation-sealed mini-palace for the Lord, a replica of His heavenly throne, through which He could speak to mankind through His priests—*mediators.*

On the seventh day, God's glory-cloud appeared and rested in His new house, with His people, the stars of heaven, arranged in perfect constellations around His new Creation.

Day 7 is the Day of the Lord. This means rest for the righteous and judgment for the wicked.

COMMENTS

The Lord's glory-cloud appears many times in the Bible. It is His "chariot." In Ezekiel 1, we are given a full description. But many times there is only a hint given of its presence, such as a mighty, rushing wind.

THE GATE OF GOD

The construction materials of the Tabernacle increase in glory (and weight) to indicate increasing holiness. The outer materials are skin, cloth and wood. The metals are bronze, then silver. The furniture in the Holy Place is covered in gold. Finally, in the Most Holy Place, everything is covered in more highly refined gold, and the lid of the Ark (the footstool of God's throne) is solid gold.

The poles and pillars indicate a symbolic multi-story building. The outer silver and gold pillars had bronze bases, and the inner gold pillars had silver bases. Covered in skins and surrounded by a "glory-cloud" robe of tents as His city, the Tabernacle was a portable tower, the heavenly blueprint measured out *story by story* on the Land.

It was the true Babel, the "gate of God," an image of the heavenly temple.

A METAL MAN

As the church is God's house and also the body of Christ, the Tabernacle is also a man, a glorious metal man.

But He is a *cruciform* man. In His left hand is the broken bread and poured out wine of Servanthood. In His right hand are the seven stars of Dominion (Revelation 1:16). The Ark is His head of gold (see Songs 5:11). The incense smoke is His elder-prayer in response to God. The Altar is His stomach, where He dines with mankind. The Laver is the living water of the Spirit pouring from His belly that washes us, the crystal sea that brings resurrection to Adam at the gate.

When Solomon's Temple replaced the Tabernacle, everything was more glorious. Among the enhancements and additions were two great bronze pillars at the entrance. The glorified Christ is seen in visions with legs of molten bronze, or a fiery, angelic stream that reaches down to the Altar of the Land. The Tabernacle was a "flying" chariot of God. When it finally rested upon the mountain of God as the Temple, these two pillars were its "landing gear."

The outer curtains of the Tabernacle were a garment for God to protect Him from the corrupt world—and a firmament to protect the corrupt world from Him. The violet and white curtain presented a two-tiered army of cherubim looking inside and outside the Tabernacle. In this glorious body, enrobed and guarded by His priests, Christ led His people through the wilderness.

Like the Garden of Eden, the Tabernacle was entered from the east, and to approach the throne, one moved west. From crucifixion to ascension, the ministry of Christ symbolically moved east-west.

Images from www.the-tabernacle-place.com. Used by permission.

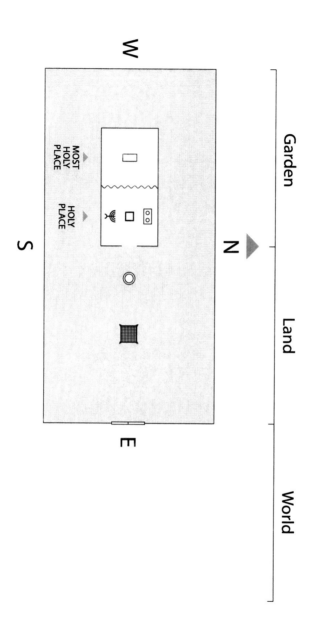

15

JOSHUA

THE FESTIVALS PATTERN puts the destruction of Jericho at Atonement. The Lord had told Abraham that the people inhabiting the Promised Land would be given more time, but now their time was up.

There was also a change in the government, from an administration of angels to a proto-administration of men. This time, it would not be angels taking life as the hosts of God, the destroyers at Passover. It would be the "resurrected" people of God. At Passover, the Hebrews passed under the sword, asleep like Adam. At Atonement, unlike Adam, they themselves were qualified to wield the "flaming sword" of the Lord as they entered the Land.

Joshua *symbolically* became the Captain of the Lord's Armies—the High Priest—and Rahab the prostitute *symbolically* became the first goat of Atonement that ascended to God as a pleasing aroma.

COMMENTS

Notice the symmetry between the first **Passover** and its first celebration in the Promised Land. There is also a correspondence between the covering blood of the **Passover** lamb (or kid) on the doorposts, and the red cord on Rahab's window (the crystal sea/Laver of **Atonement**).

If the Tabernacle imagery is applied, we see that at **Firstfruits** the people are sacrifices on the Bronze Altar, and they failed to enter the Land. But at **Trumpets**, being more mature, they are elders, incense on the Golden Altar. This "promotion" was the purpose of the wilderness.

The seventh feast is often called Tabernacles, but throughout this book I call it **Booths**. The Hebrew word for **Booths** *(succoth)* also means "clouds." God initiates the pattern with a creative Word from His glory-cloud, and it ends with redeemed mankind, recreated in God's image as His "corporate" glory-cloud. Our "individual" clouds are the robes of glory we forfeited in Adam. They are the robes of transfigured wise men who judge angels—a corporate mediator. Consequently, the seventh book concerns the *Judges*.

THE DOMINION OF ISRAEL

Creation - **Sabbath:**
God brings an end to slavery under Pharaoh

Division - **Passover:**
Believers are separated from Egypt

Ascension - **Firstfruits:**
A new people is brought to God

Testing - **Pentecost:**
The Law is given. Israel is tested

Maturity - **Trumpets:**
A new army is brought to God

Conquest - **Atonement:**
Passover is celebrated in the Promised Land.
Rahab is separated. Jericho is destroyed. The
Land is divided among the tribes, who rule
their territories under God

Glorification - **Booths:**
Adam's rest. The people dwell with God, feast
and drink wine in the land of milk, honey, oil
and wine

JUDGES

THE FIRST SEVEN BOOKS OF THE BIBLE follow the general themes of the seven days of Creation.

- *Genesis* - God establishes light in the midst of darkness
- *Exodus* - He separates a people for God
- *Leviticus* - A new priesthood draws near to God in a newly-**form**ed house
- *Numbers* - The children of Israel, as a cosmic host, travel through the sky from Egypt to the Promised Land
- *Deuteronomy* - An army "swarms" to **fill** the Land
- *Joshua* - Adam and Eve are brought to rest in the garden of the Promised Land

Joshua ends with the death of Eleazar, the son of Aaron. At the death of the High Priest, it was safe for all those protected in cities of refuge to return home (Booths). After committing to obey the Lord, every man returned to his inheritance. Everyone was in their own Garden of God, like Adam.

- *Judges* - As Day 7, this book expands on what happened after Adam was given the Garden

In the time of Judges, Israel was now *Glorified*. The people were living in God's Land, but after Joshua died, the priests failed to serve at the throne and feed the people. Both worship and morality deteriorated, so the Lord allowed the nations to discipline those who had forsaken the true *Baal* ("lord") for Canaanite fakes.

Our culture reflects our worship, and Israel would learn firsthand about the nature of the cultures that resulted from their new gods.

Although there are twelve judges mentioned in the book, there were **seven elected judges**: Othniel, Ehud, Deborah, Gideon, Abimelech, Jephthah, and Samson.

These books are often strange to our modern ears, but they contain themes that echo throughout the rest of the Bible.

COMMENTS

There is way too much ground to cover here for this little book, but we can observe some general themes.

Notice that Deborah, the "judgess," appears at the Covenant step, reflecting Adam's marriage to Eve. Christ said He saw Satan fall like "lightning," which occurred when Christ Himself ascended to the Father and threw down the usurper.

Gideon is a "feller of trees" in the garden of *Testing*. In the Gideon narrative, as **Pentecost/Lampstand**, the Lord's armies break jars of clay to expose burning lamps which confuse and defeat his enemies.

Jephthah's daughter symbolically ascends to the mountain of God—through the Laver—as a living sacrifice.

Creation - *Othniel* ("lion/might/power of God").
Defeated the "flood" of Mesopotamian invaders
from "proto-Babylon" *(Sabbath)*

> **Division** - Ehud ("united"). Divided with a
> blade and then locked the kingdom doors on
> Eglon the Sodomite king *(Passover)*

> > **Ascension** - *Deborah* ("bee")
> > and *Barak* ("lightning"). The "seed" (Barak)
> > of the Woman (Deborah) crushed the head
> > of the "seed" (Sisera) of the serpent (Jabin)
> > *(Firstfruits)*

> > > **Testing** - *Gideon* ("feller of trees").
> > > Opened the flaming eyes of God among
> > > His enemies *(Pentecost)*

> > **Maturity** - *Abimelech* ("my father is king").
> > Slew his brothers and assembled an idola-
> > trous army *(Trumpets)*

> **Conquest** - *Jephthah* ("he will free/break
> through"). Defeated Ammon, but because he
> was illegitimate, could not become king.
> Because of his vow, his daughter ascended to
> the mountain of God *(Atonement)*

Glorification - *Samson* ("sun/sunrise").
The mighty bridegroom who destroyed the false
temple. He was the *Glorification* answer to the
Ascension prayer of Deborah (Judges 5:31), wine
from her grain and fruit plants *(Booths)*

145

RUTH

BECAUSE OF THE FAILURE OF THE PRIESTHOOD, and Israel's resulting sin, the Lord sent a famine. The nation itself became a barren womb.

The Lord used a Gentile bride—*a bride from outside*—to bring a king from the barren womb of Israel. Ruth—Day 8—is the beginning of a new cycle for the nation. Ruth is about the raising of a new prophet, a servant-king.

COMMENTS

Again, the sons of God saw that the daughters of men were good (Genesis 6), and again it occurs at the centre of the cycle. This time it is Ruth that "enters" the Covenant ark, with Orpah left outside. The two women are the divided "body," the twin goats of **Atonement**.

In the book of Ruth, by the birth of David, the houses of Moab and Judah are redeemed from being illegitimate.

● **De-Creation** - God brings famine upon the Land *(Sabbath)*

● **Division** - Elimelech abandons the Covenant and makes a false exodus *(Passover)*

○ **Ascension** - The true *House of Bread (Beth-Lehem)* Tabernacle is abandoned for the fields of the Moabites, who had denied bread and water to Israel in the wilderness, and with whose women Israel had committed adultery *(Firstfruits)*

◉ **Testing** - The daughters of Israel are abandoned for the daughters of Lot (Moabite women) *(Pentecost)*

◉ **Maturity** - Naomi decides to return to the House of Bread *(Beth-Lehem) (Trumpets)*

◐ **Conquest** - Orpah and Ruth are separated, and Ruth and Naomi enter the Promised Land *(Atonement)*

● **Glorification** - Boaz fulfills the Levirate Law and marries Ruth, who gives birth to a "surrogate" son, Obed, on Naomi's lap. The Covenant is restored and fulfilled. Israel is made fruitful again through the faithfulness of Boaz and the Gentile "riches" of redeemed Ruth. The book ends with her godly offspring, David *(Booths)*

18

SAMUEL

THE OLD HOUSE OF MOSES, a temporary tent of cloth and skins, was decaying and ready to pass away, and the new house of David, a permanent house of stone, was promised.

Eli the High Priest failed to raise godly offspring, and his two sons, like the sons of Aaron, were unfaithful priests. The abuse in the house of God was the source of the nation's oppression, so Eli's house would be cut off. According to the Law, the Land would spit out the Covenant-breakers.

But the Lord Himself, their rejected King, carried the curse in their place: Israel had become Egypt so the Ark itself headed for the wilderness, taken captive by the Philistines.

The Lord will always let His own reputation suffer rather than allow His unrepentant people to manipulate Him. The Ark would return (and with Gentile singers)—only once a new Tabernacle had been established in the "city of peace"—*Jerusalem.*

COMMENTS

Dagon, as a sea beast, was covered in scales. This "serpent" lost his head at the centre of the cycle.

The use of the exodus pattern effectively makes this cycle the creation of a new Covenant.

The wise judge at the end of the cycle is Samuel, but like Eli, his ungodly offspring were rejected. Israel requested *Glorification* before time and ended up with a king like the Gentiles.

Notice that the house of Moses ended as it began—with Egyptian plagues and plunder: the Philistines were descendants of the Egyptians. Notice also that the Philistines made the plunder into the shape of ten plagues: five golden tumors and five golden rats.

Creation - Israel attempts to defeat the Philistines at Aphek using the Ark as a magic charm *(Sabbath)*

Division - Phinehas and Hophni, the sons of Eli, are slain *(Passover)*

Ascension - Eli *hears* the news, *falls* from his seat and *dies*. The Ark is stolen by the Philistines and placed in the temple of Dagon *(Firstfruits)*

Testing - Dagon falls down before the Ark, is restored, then falls again and is broken in pieces *(Pentecost)*

Maturity - The Lord defeats the Philistines with terrible plagues and returns with a plunder of gold. The Ark never returns to the Tabernacle. The house of Moses is ended *(Trumpets)*

Conquest - Samuel takes over as Joshua did, Israel separates from their idols, and the Philistines are defeated at Ebenezer *(Atonement)*

Glorification - Blind Eli is replaced by Samuel the "seer," but his sons are wisely rejected. Israel unwisely requests a human king *(Booths)*

19

SAUL

SAUL SINNED IN THE *Garden*, failing to wait seven days for Samuel to make the sacrifice. He sinned in the *Land*, making a rash vow that kept food from his men and threatened the life of his son Jonathan. And his sin in the *World*, styling himself as a Gentile king and friend to Amalek (the Lord's sworn enemy), forced the Lord to reject him. His kingdom would be taken away.

COMMENTS

Jonathan is the godly offspring at *Ascension* and *Glorification*.

Maturity is the step where the Gentiles are brought into the Covenant, but Saul had compromised with them. The "Incense Altar" government was transferred.

As with Joshua, David here is symbolically the High Priest, the mediating Adam, who had "holy to the Lord" engraved into the hard, gold plate on his forehead. What David did to Goliath's forehead pictured Jesus' head-crushing victory over the serpent.

Notice that Saul's initial victory over the Philistines is matched with David's victory over Goliath. Saul failed to overcome the Philistines' monopoly over iron weapons. David used the Philistine's iron weapon against him.

Creation - Saul is anointed with oil by Samuel the prophet *(Sabbath)*

Division - **Bad exodus:** After Saul's victory over the Philistines, he fails to wait for sacrifice (death). The Philistines dominate with a monopoly of iron and their oppression increases *(Passover)*

Ascension - **Bad priesthood:** Saul withholds food from his soldiers, and they eat meat with the blood, which puts them under a Covenant curse. His son Jonathan's life is threatened because he partook of a Covenant blessing (honey) *(Firstfruits)*

Testing - **Bad serpent-killing:** Saul defeats the Amalekites but fellowships with a Gentile king, Agag, and keeps the devoted plunder *(Pentecost)*

Maturity - **Bad government:** Samuel rejects Saul's house and tears his robe. Saul has no Gentile sponsor. The responsibility falls back from king and priest to prophet, and Samuel cuts Agag to pieces. David is anointed in his place *(Trumpets)*

Conquest - Although Saul is tall, and a Benjaminite (good with a slingshot, Judges 20:16), he is afraid. It is David who is willing to stand alone and kill Goliath *(Atonement)*

Glorification - Jonathan abdicates by making a Covenant with David, giving him his armor and robe. Saul becomes Pharaoh, a tyrant king. Israel is forced to wait another decade for a king after God's heart *(Booths)*

20

DAVID

SAUL AND DAVID WERE ANOINTED BY SAMUEL, and he was like a father to both of them. Like Cain and Abel, Ishmael and Isaac, Jacob and Esau, Judah and Joseph, Elimelech and Boaz, the Lord once again used a faithful *younger brother* to replace a disqualified elder brother. The rivalry would intensify after Samuel's death. Saul, like Herod, would attempt to murder the legitimate king.

David could have become like Saul, but the Lord used Saul's persecution to bring David's faith to maturity. Oppressed saints who retaliate often become even more inclined to throw spears than their oppressors. In Judges and 1 Samuel, the weapons used to defeat the enemy reflected the ordinary people who used them: a tent peg, an ox goad, a millstone, an ass's jawbone, a slingshot. It was Saul who started throwing spears like a Gentile, like Goliath.

David, however, humbled himself like Joseph and was exalted in due time. The eighth son of Jesse was a new Creation.

COMMENTS

The battle was fought by one representative from each army, typifying the battle between Christ and Satan at the cross.

Just as Satan was the Accuser of God's people, Goliath called down the Covenant curses upon Israel.

As a false "Temple," Goliath's legs were covered in bronze armor. Like his god, Dagon, he was covered in scales (chainmail) and "broken in pieces" before the new Ark-king, David.

Goliath's head was removed and taken to Jerusalem. It is possibly the reason for the name of the site of the crucifixion, the place of the skull.

○ **Creation** - Jesse's seven eldest sons are rejected. David, Jesse's eighth son, is anointed by Samuel. He is the first day of a new week *(Sabbath)*

❧ **Division** - David receives the Spirit, but Saul receives an evil spirit (substitutionary death) *(Passover)*

○ **Ascension** - David shepherds Jesse's sheep, and feeds his brothers in the "wilderness." Riches, the king's daughter and a house (Tabernacle) of freedom are promised *(Firstfruits)*

◉ **Testing** - Saul's army is paralyzed by fear in the "wilderness." After 40 days of taunts, David kills Goliath, the serpent *(Pentecost)*

❧ **Maturity** - The Land is reclaimed, and the Philistines are plundered. David lives permanently in the king's house, and Jonathan becomes his brother by Covenant. Jonathan gives David his robe, and David is set over the men of war *(Trumpets)*

❧ **Conquest** - David escapes Saul's spear (resurrection) and misses out on Saul's elder daughter. David kills two hundred Philistines and marries Saul's younger daughter, Michal *(Atonement)*

○ **Glorification** - David's fame overtakes that of Saul. Saul is symbolically "uncircumcised" *(Booths)*

Many of the seven-point cycles in Bible history have a small cycle that prefigures a large one. We observed this with the capture of the Ark by the Philistines. It was a small version of a greater picture. The Ark was returned by the Philistines but was never returned to the Tabernacle. There was a good reason for this: the reign of Saul.

Saul was tested in Garden, Land and World, and, like Adam, failed because of his impatience for glory. Not only this, but when David returned the Ark to Jerusalem, Michal mocked him, and the Lord made this daughter of Saul *barren*. The Ark, which had been out of the Tabernacle for the entire reign of Saul, had borne the curse for the corrupted Levite priesthood. The Covenant curses fell upon the apostate king, and he was beheaded (cut in two) and hung high to be symbolically eaten by demons (unclean birds).

With the Ark's return, David restructured the priesthood, adding twenty-four chief priests under the High Priest. He also incorporated Gentile worshippers and music. This resurrected "Tabernacle of David" was a new body—a bride prepared for a marriage which would occur when Solomon's permanent house of God, the Temple, was complete.

COMMENTS

The Ark's exile removed the false **priesthood**. The Ark's return removed the dynasty of the false **king**. We shall see this factor repeated in both the Babylonian captivity and the New Testament.

   Creation - Ark taken (house of Eli removed)

   Division - Ark exiled in Philistia

    Ascension - Ark returned on a cart,
    instead of being carried by authorized
    men (sin regarding ark)

     Testing - Ark with Abinadab

The restoration of the Ark to the centre of Israel's religious and national life does not take place until after David's conquest of Jerusalem. The sequence of events in the ascension of the ark to Zion exactly reverses the events of the ark's removal from the Mosaic tabernacle:

    Maturity - Ark returned on a cart,
    instead of being carried by authorized
    men (sin regarding ark)

   Conquest - Ark housed with a Philistine

   Glorification - Ark Restored (house of Saul removed)[1]

---

1 This chiasm is from Peter J. Leithart, *Death and Resurrection of the Tabernacle*, BIBLICAL HORIZONS No. 114, www.biblicalhorizons.com

David's greatest sin could have made him like Saul—
he started seizing things. His twin sins of adultery and
murder violated both his role as servant-king before
the throne of God, and his role as a priest to the
Gentiles. Reflecting this more advanced stage in Israel's
growth towards maturity, judgment was not an
immediate "spanking" as it had been in the wilderness,
but the experience and suffering of the long term
consequences of sin.

David's first error was a refusal to enter into *Testing*,
but the chiasm shows that although the first three steps
were negative, David's repentance turned things
around. The Word of the Lord to David through
Nathan the prophet is the hero of the story. It was a
light to his path in the wilderness, a lamp(stand) to his
feet (Psalm 119:105).

COMMENTS

The Old Covenant priests were armed for the purpose
of defending the Sanctuary. Those who took the Nazirite
vow became a kind of temporary priest. Notice that
David covers his failure to go to war with a false sacrifice.

DOMINION COMMANDED OVER AMMON

- **Creation** - (Disobedience) David rebels against his anointing and remains in Jerusalem instead of going to "holy war"

  - **Division** - (Union) David seizes Bathsheba and sleeps with her. As a false prophet, he tries to cover his own sin by calling Uriah home to his wife (death)

    - **Ascension** - (Betrayal) As a false priest, David offers Uriah's life (the Gentile convert) for his own

      - **Testing** - (Serpent) Nathan, as God's *Lampstand* eyes, challenges the deceiver

    - **Maturity** - David repents and retains the throne

  - **Conquest** - The son as the scapegoat dies in David's place. David stops mourning, then washes and anoints himself (resurrection)

- **Glorification** - Solomon is born to build God's house

DAVID WEARS THE CROWN OF AMMON

21

SOLOMON

BECAUSE OF DAVID'S SIN, there had been enemies on every side and no rest for the king. Peace would only come with the prince of peace. Solomon's reign brought Israel into the Sabbath of Tabernacles under the wisest judge who ever lived.

The beginning of Solomon's reign is not only a new Creation, but symbolically a reconquest of the Land.

COMMENTS

Notice that the account situates Solomon's marriage as a true Covenant, but the two prostitutes as "the daughters of men." Solomon initially demonstrates wise judgment concerning women, both in marriage and in court. As a faithful witness to the Gentiles, Solomon changed the world around him, but it wasn't to last.

Creation - Solomon is anointed king by Zadok the priest and Nathan the prophet *(Sabbath)*

Division - There is an "attack on the bride" (Abishag the concubine) and the death of the son (Adonijah). Enemies of Solomon are destroyed in a single wave *(Passover)*

Ascension - Solomon marries Pharaoh's daughter. The Lord renews the Covenant in a dream *(Firstfruits)*

Testing - Solomon judges the two mothers, the false and the true (like Hagar and Sarah). Solomon wisely discerns which is "barren" by the true mother's love for the living child *(Pentecost)*

Maturity - Solomon's officials are listed and his government is established *(Trumpets)*

Conquest - Solomon sets twelve officers over the Land of Israel (as Joshua dividing the inheritance) *(Atonement)*

Glorification - Judah and Israel eat and drink and are happy. Solomon rules over all the Land promised to Abraham. With the kingdom at rest, he builds a permanent house for the Lord *(Booths)*

As the Tabernacle instructions follow the Creation Week pattern, so does the description of the forming and filling of the Temple—a new cosmos, a new Creation (1 Kings 6-8).

Sabbath - Land at rest

Passover - Doors covered (death)

Firstfruits - Sinai ascended.
Adam presented to God

Pentecost - Tabernacle constructed for the king

Trumpets - Armies mustered.
Eve presented to God

Atonement - Doors opened (resurrection)

Booths - Adam and Eve are united with God

COMMENTS

At *Maturity*, the plunder from Gentile nations is brought into the Temple. You might notice that Ruth symbolized the riches of faithful Gentiles brought into the Covenant people.

Day 1 - **Forming heavens and earth:** With the Land at rest, Solomon builds a three-story house. The Word of the Lord reminds Solomon of the Covenant conditions. Light and darkness are separated—the Most Holy Place is separated and lined with gold *(Sabbath)*

Day 2 - **Forming firmament:** The olive wood doors to the inner sanctuary and the cypress doors to the nave are constructed, carved with cherubim (guarding priests) and palm trees (judging kings) as guardians of the throne *(Passover)*

Day 3 - **Forming land:** The Temple as the altar/mountain of God is completed after seven years *(Firstfruits)*

Day 4 - **Filling heaven:** Now Solomon's palace complex is built, a new firmament house for the sun and moon rulers, Solomon and his wife *(Pentecost)*

Day 5 - **Filling firmament:** The Temple furniture is constructed: the bronze pillars, the Laver/sea and the ten bronze chariots, the Altar of Incense, ten Lampstands, and the Table of Showbread. The plunder devoted to the Temple by David is also brought in *(Trumpets)*

Day 6 - **Filling land:** The doors are opened. Animals are sacrificed, and the priests bring the Ark into the Most Holy Place *(Atonement)*

Day 7 - **Shekinah:** The glory of the Lord enters and rests in the Temple. Solomon as mediator faces the Lord, then faces man, and heaven and earth are one—the ultimate Sabbath *(Booths)*

As a glorified Adam, Solomon ate from the Tree of Wisdom, formed and filled a new Creation (Ecclesiastes 2), "named" the animals (1 Kings 4:33), and extended his dominion from the Garden/Temple, across Israel (Land) to the ends of his prototype World (Havilah).

The rich are subject to temptations that the poor will never know, which explains the Lord's three special commands for kings (Deuteronomy 17:14-20). Solomon broke all three of these laws. He collected 666 talents of gold every year, built an army of chariots and horses (some from Egypt) and fell for the "daughters of men," pagan wives who would entice him to sacrifice to their false gods on the mountain "east of Jerusalem"—the Mount of Olives. Sex, money and power, or girls, gold and guns. As with David's sin, the consequences of the king's sin were long term.

Here is the *Creation* and *De-Creation* of Solomon's kingdom, with Solomon as the sun-ruler at the centre.

COMMENTS

At **Firstfruits**, church and state are united in the obedient king. Matching this at **Trumpets**, the true church has been removed from the city. New worship always starts from scratch in the wilderness. Jesus was crucified *outside the city*.

PROPHET:

Creation - Ark: In the Garden/Temple, Israel receives the heavenly pattern to be measured out—the Word of God *(Sabbath)*

> PRIEST:
>
> **Division - Veil:** In the Land, Israel mediates between God and the nations, when faithful to the Word *(Passover)*
>
> > KING:
> >
> > **Ascension - Altar and Table:** In the World, Israel has a united kingdom with the king as prophet and priest *(Firstfruits)*
> >
> > > DOMINION:
> > >
> > > **Testing - Lampstand:** After Solomon commits idolatry, *(Pentecost)*
> >
> > ANTI-KING:
> >
> > **Maturity - Incense Altar:** prophets bring warnings to the various kings. The kingdom is *divided (un-Trumpets)*
>
> ANTI-PRIEST:
>
> **Conquest - High Priest:** The idolatry continues and the priesthood becomes *corrupted, (un-Atonement)*

ANTI-PROPHET:

Glorification - Shekinah Glory: Finally, the glory departs (Ezekiel 10-11) and the Temple is left unprotected. It is *destroyed* by Gentiles, the armies of Babylon *(un-Booths)*

Jeremiah was branded a false prophet for bringing the word from the Lord to obey the king of Babylon. The last king of Judah, Zedekiah, ignored Jeremiah's warnings, and his fate says it all. In Babylon, his sons were slain before his eyes, which were then put out, and like Samson, he became a slave. Israel's "Sabbath-kings" had behaved like the brutal, idolatrous Gentile kings, so the Lord raised Nebuchadnezzar as His glorified servant-king (Jeremiah 25:9).

Ironically, it was Nebuchadnezzar, a *real* Gentile king who brought rest to the Land—70 years of Sabbaths that were overdue. The Gentile "70" also makes this a mockery of the Feast of Booths: Israel herself was the food on the table as the unclean scavengers came to glut themselves.

With the lion of Judah dethroned, God would use the winged lion-cherub of Babylon to purify and guard the "woman," the mother of the true Sabbath king— the promised Saviour.

COMMENTS

Again, we have a smaller cycle, then a larger one. The first cycle covers the split of the kingdom and the establishment of the Northern Kingdom. Just like Solomon, Jeroboam was given the kingdom by the Lord, with the usual Covenant blessings for obedience and Covenant curses for disobedience.

Creation - *Sabbath removed:* Solomon's throne becomes a "high place" of false worship. The Lord "anoints" adversaries for Solomon: an Edomite, a Gentile and Jeroboam the Ephraimite. Ahijah the prophet tears his robe into twelve pieces and gives ten of them to Jeroboam

> **Division** - *Kingdom split:* Like Pharaoh, Solomon's son Rehoboam doubles the workload of the people, resulting in a revolt, with Jeroboam crowned king of the northern tribes. Rehoboam remains king of the south, Judah

>> **Ascension** - *False worship established:* Like Aaron, Jeroboam sets up golden calves to appease the people. He appoints non-Levite priests, builds his own altar and even names his sons after Aaron's sons whom the Lord killed for offering strange fire

>>> **Testing** - *The eyes of the Lord:* Like Nathan, a prophet confronts the serpent-king. He promises a son of David who will tear down the false worship—King Josiah

>> **Maturity** - *Trumpet warnings:* The Lord sends the two signs as witnesses: Jeroboam's withered hand, and the deception and death of the prophet. Jeroboam continues in his sin, and Ahijah brings the curses of the Covenant upon his house

> **Conquest** - *Sin covered:* His son dies at the door

Glorification - *Ungodly offspring:* Jeroboam dies and is replaced by his son, Nadab

COMMENTS

Like Nathan, the prophets were lawyers sent by the Lord with "Covenant lawsuits" against the kings. They were the "**Pentecost**" eyes of the Lord, exposing sin. Their voices were "**Trumpets**" warning a kingdom of God that had become like Jericho. This time, however, the armies were not the soldiers of Israel. They were the Gentile Sea flooding over the Altar-Land to "drown" the disobedient "sons of God."

Here you can see the larger pattern, ending with a new Sabbath for the oppressed people of Judah, the poor who were left in the Land by Nebuchadnezzar to keep the vineyards. As with Noah's flood, the cycle ends with a new king, a new Law and a purified Land—and a vineyard.

Creation - Solomon's throne becomes a "high place" of false worship

Division - The Lord divides his kingdom

Ascension - The priesthood becomes corrupt

Testing - The prophets challenge the kings

Maturity - The armies of Assyria and Babylon are summoned by God to destroy His people. The various Gentile invasions are like the plagues brought by Moses upon Egypt (Jeremiah 21:7)

Conquest - Finally, Nebuchadnezzar destroys Jerusalem and the Temple, just as Joshua brought down Jericho (2 Chronicles 36)

Glorification - The wicked are taken into captivity, but the Land itself is given all the Sabbaths owed to it. The last "Solomon" king of Judah is *unwise* Zedekiah. His *sons* are slain before his eyes and then he is *blinded* (2 Kings 25:7)

NEBU-CHADNEZZAR

IN THE NORTHERN KINGDOM, only one dynasty lasted longer than four generations (Jehu), and their last king only ruled for six months. All the northern kings were bad. In Judah, however, the house of David ruled continuously with only the one interruption—the false reign of Athaliah. God kept His promise.

Hezekiah's son Manasseh reconstructed the icons his father had destroyed. He built altars for all the armies of heaven (the stars) in the two courts of the house of the Lord. He burned his sons as sacrifices and consulted witches. Israel followed his leadership and became *worse* than the Canaanites. Like Jeroboam in the north, Manasseh's name became a proverb for the source of idolatry in the south. However, the Lord had other plans for this king. He would personally prefigure both the captivity *and* Restoration of Israel.

The Lord uses the Garden, Land, World pattern consistently. Judgment begins at the house of God. The Word comes from the sanctuary, bringing about events among the people of God. Eventually the shockwaves reach the entire world.

The account of Judah's idolatrous King Manasseh gives us a *personal* picture of the shape of Israel's *national* experience later on. As in Leviticus 1, the head of the sacrifice is offered first, then the body. In this case, it was both a warning and a promise, a curse and a blessing. The King of Israel *was* the Covenant.

COMMENTS

The book of Jonah follows a similar pattern, with the prophet "in the belly of the beast" at the centre of the cycle.

Just as the Ark defeated Dagon when captive in Philistia, here the false god that was broken was Manasseh's idolatrous heart.

Creation - The Lord speaks to Manasseh but is ignored...

Division - ...so He brings the Assyrians, who put a hook in his nose and take him captive in chains to Babylon

> **Ascension** - Manasseh humbles himself before the God of his fathers, and the Lord is moved

> > **Testing** - "Then Manasseh knew that the Lord was God"

> **Maturity** - Manasseh is returned to Jerusalem, and he builds a very high outer wall for the city

Conquest - He puts commanders in all the fortified cities of Judah and throws the idols from the Temple

Glorification - Manasseh commands a restoration of true worship

COMMENTS

This pattern of the death and resurrection of Israel, via the "belly of the beast" in Babylon, is a crucial overview to understand. It is the foundation for the events of the first century, recorded in the New Testament.

Creation - The Lord warns Israel through the prophets

Division - Nebuchadnezzar takes the ruling classes and tradesmen captive into his "household"

Ascension - In captivity, Daniel *ascends* to the right hand of Nebuchadnezzar as an advisor to the king. In captivity, the Lord *anoints* Ezekiel as a new High Priest for the captives. These men are two witnesses against Jerusalem. The Lord gives the command to destroy His "Tabernacle"

Testing - Nebuchadnezzar (presumably, with Daniel's advice) destroys Jerusalem, and the Jews repent of their idolatry forever

Maturity - Through Cyrus the Great, the Lord gives the command to rebuild. Under Ezra, captives are returned to Jerusalem and the Altar is rebuilt. Under Nehemiah, the wall is rebuilt. The prophets Haggai and Zechariah bring about the completion of the new Temple. Joshua and Zerubbabel represent a new priesthood and a new kingdom united in a single High Priestly crown

Conquest - This is where the events of the book of Esther take place. Once Haman is executed, Mordecai takes command as advisor to the Persian king. An empire-wide battle subdues a greater Land for God's people than Joshua could have imagined

Glorification - The plunder from this conquest adorns the new Temple. But this Temple is just a token: the true plunder is people who submit to the Covenant, which explains the fulfillment of Ezekiel's Temple vision. It is a Temple made of people

COMMENTS

Looking back, we can see that the structure of the book of Ezekiel not only follows the Egypt to Canaan events under Moses, but echoes the cycle of Adam to Noah. At the centre of the cycle are the "mighty men," the Canaanite nations around Israel who benefited from alliances with the Covenant people and were made strong.

Creation - Ezekiel is anointed as High Priest, a Lampstand with flaming eyes, a burning bush in the wilderness (Ezekiel 1-7)

Division - "Egypt" is inspected, and the destroyers bring a city-wide Passover (Ezekiel 8-11)

Ascension - Solomon's Temple is deconstructed in a *De-Creation* pattern (Ezekiel 12-24)

Testing - Solomon's wives, the "daughters of men" and their "mighty men" offspring (Canaanite nations) are judged in the wilderness (Ezekiel 25-32). As Tyre, Solomon's gold was stolen by foreigners. As Sidon, his oppressive taxation was cut off. And as Egypt, his many wives were taken captive, and his imported horses were drowned in the Sea

Maturity - The Law is repeated, the Covenant is renewed, and the houses of Israel and Judah that were divided after Solomon are reunited. Esau is expelled (Ezekiel 33-36)

Conquest - The nation is resurrected as a united army. Haman, a descendant of Agag (Gog), is defeated by Mordecai, of the family of Saul (Kish). It is a reconquest of the Promised Land (Ezekiel 37-39)

Glorification - A new Temple is measured out, but the east gate is shut until the Greater Solomon (Jesus) enters to eat with God (Ezekiel 40-48)

The Babylonian empire was a "flood" that not only swallowed up idolatrous Israel, but also the Canaanite nations surrounding it. Only the Jews resurfaced—a resurrected priestly altar. If they were faithful witnesses, they would "ascend" to rule alongside the Gentile emperors. The empires were not a burden for Israel as many think, but a *promotion*. The Lord had scattered Israel for disobedience, but would now give her greater dominion as a nation of priests—*mediators*. Synagogues were established right across the empire, and we see the results of this ministry in the many Gentile believers encountered by the Apostles in the book of Acts. Without a Davidic king, the new role of Israel was prophetic. It required even greater wisdom.

With the Persian empire under the rule of Mordecai and Esther, the prophecy of Noah was fulfilled. The sons of Ham were forever disempowered, and the sons of Shem now ruled a greater territory. This is the meaning of Ezekiel's Temple. The empires were an ark that would carry Israel into the New Covenant world.

But again, this structure would not last. As in the book of Judges, the people of God would fail to dominate this empire-Land. When the Gentile "Pharaoh" forgot the Shemite "Josephs" (Daniel and Mordecai), the Jews again ended up in slavery for 400 years. This is the time between the end of the Old Testament and the New. The entire process of death and resurrection would be repeated one final time for the sake of the sons of Japheth. The Garden (Israel) passed through death and resurrection, then the empire-Land. All that remained was the World.

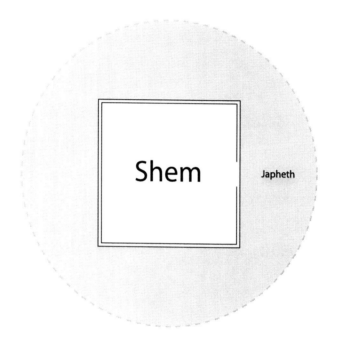

23

ISRAEL

JAMES JORDAN CLAIMS THAT THE GENTILE EMPIRES were an ark that would carry Israel across the waters of the flood into a New Covenant world. This is supported by the structure of Israel's history, which places these events at Old Covenant Israel's Day 6.

On Day 6, the Lord created Land animals and Man. Daniel 7 uses Land animals walking on water as symbols of the four Gentile empires: Babylon, Persia, Greece and Rome. They are like the four-faced cherubim surrounding God's throne above the crystal sea, beasts supporting the enthroned Man, who appears later in the chapter.

Once Christ came as the perfect Adam, the true Mediator, He ascended to rule over the "animal" kingdoms, naming them in a New Creation. Then the Father gave Him a Bride. The Christian church was Israel's Day 7.

COMMENTS

Notice that this pattern makes the ministry of the prophets the "two witnesses," Moses and Aaron, while the armies of Assyria and Babylon are the plagues upon an Israel that became just like the Egypt the Lord had rescued her from.

The Lord's call to Peter to receive Gentiles into the church using an image of unclean animals also begins to make more sense. The captivity scattered Israel like seed, and Acts shows a harvest of many Gentile God-fearers who grew from the synagogue ministry of the Jews. God gathered them into the body of Christ.

DAY 1 - LIGHT
Creation - PATRIARCHS, ABRAHAM
Light dawns upon the "waters" of the 70 nations

DAY 2 - WATERS
Division - EXODUS, MOSES
Israel is separated to mediate for the nations

DAY 3 - DRY LAND
Ascension - PROMISED LAND, JOSHUA
Israel is "resurrected" to rule upon the Land

DAY 4 - RULING LIGHTS
Testing - SAMUEL, DAVID & SOLOMON
Mighty men conquer the Canaanites

DAY 5 - SWARMS
Maturity - CAPTIVITY, NEBUCHADNEZZAR
The prophets witness to the kings. Gentile armies
plague the Land and Sea as eagles and sea
monsters

DAY 6 - MAN
Conquest - RESTORATION, JOSHUA THE
HIGH PRIEST TO "JOSHUA" THE CHRIST
Israel is again separated to mediate for the nations,
working as a priesthood within a Gentile "ark"

DAY 7 - REST
Glorification - JESUS AND THE CHURCH
Christ comes as the Lord on Day 7 to judge the
Land and destroy the Herods' false temple. But He
is also a faithful Adam who feasts with His bride in
a new house. Booths (Tabernacles) is fulfilled

24

JESUS

WITH THE ARRIVAL OF THE PROMISED SAVIOUR, human history moved into the next phase. As Man, God stepped in to face the tempter in Adam's place.

With His success, the white fields could begin to be harvested. Jesus became the Sun of Righteousness on Day 4 at the centre of history.

Creation - A world united as one blood *(Sabbath)*

Division - A world divided by blood *(Passover)*

Ascension - A centralized priesthood *(Firstfruits)*

Testing - The harvest begins *(Pentecost)*

Solomon ruled the Land, and Nebuchadnezzar ruled the World. But the Lord moved His dominion strategy to the next level. Nebuchadnezzar's proto-"World" became simply a greater Land to be conquered.

With the final death-and-resurrection of Israel in the first century, the mediator at the right hand of the power would not be on earth but in heaven, ruling over the *actual* World.

COMMENTS

The gospels contain many chiastic structures, and these often overlap. There are also many instances of the Bible Matrix pattern. Notice it in the early chapters of Matthew's gospel. Harmonization between the gospels is difficult because the writers arranged their historical accounts in theological rather than chronological orders to make a point.

JESUS BEGINS HIS MINISTRY

Creation - The genealogy and birth of Jesus, the Word become flesh *(Sabbath)*

Division - The infants are slaughtered by Herod the Great. Jesus is removed, ironically, to Egypt *(Passover)*

Ascension - Jesus is baptized and rises to begin His ministry *(Firstfruits)*

Testing - Jesus is tested in the wilderness *(Pentecost)*

Maturity - John, the ultimate holy warrior, dies as a martyr/witness. But Jesus is resurrecting Israel by casting out plagues and making people ceremonially *clean*. As Moses, He preaches the Law to this new generation *(Trumpets)*

Conquest - Jesus crosses the sea in a boat. He makes it into a "crystal sea" by subduing a storm. He casts a legion of demons out of a man dwelling in the tombs (symbolic of the Most Holy Place) *(Atonement)*

Glorification - Jesus attends a supper at Matthew's house *(Booths)*

COMMENTS

Jesus brings both the blessings and curses of the Law. As *Re-Creation* and *De-Creation*, these follow the pattern of Genesis 1.

JESUS' BLESSINGS

Creation - Jesus opened His mouth and taught them. It was actually those with a humble spirit who owned the Creation (*Sabbath*)

Division - Those who set themselves apart and mourned for the sins of the Land would be comforted (*Passover*)

Ascension - The obedient would inherit the Land. Those who were hungry and thirsty for righteousness would be satisfied (*Firstfruits*)

Testing - The merciful would obtain mercy. The pure in heart would *see* God (*Pentecost*)

Maturity - The true sons of God are martyrs for unity, peacemakers (*Trumpets*)

Conquest - As the prophets were persecuted before them, so these new sons of God would be accused and rejected (*Atonement*)

Glorification - Their reward is in heaven (*Booths*)

COMMENTS

Not only does the remainder of Jesus' sermon follow the pattern, these blessings are mirrored by the curses upon the saints' "evil twins" in Matthew 23, the Jewish rulers who sat in Moses' seat of judgment. The entire book of Matthew is chiastic, and the beatitudes are mirrored negatively in these seven woes. Like all previous Covenants, the New Covenant contains both blessings and curses.

JESUS' CURSES

Creation - The scribes and Pharisees sit in Moses' seat of judgment but keep the commandments for the eyes of men *(Sabbath - Ark)*

> **Division** - Unlike Moses, they shut the doors of the kingdom of heaven in people's faces and refuse to enter in themselves *(Passover - Veil)*

> > **Ascension** - They cross *Land and Sea* to make one disciple for their corrupted religion *(Firstfruits - Altar and Table)*

> > > **Testing** - They are *blind* guides who make false oaths and teach others to do the same *(Pentecost - Lampstand)*

> > **Maturity** - Instead of being an Israel resurrected, they are whitewashed tombs. They claim to honor the murdered prophets. Jesus dares them to murder Him *(Trumpets)*

> **Conquest** - On this generation would fall the judgment for all the innocent blood shed from Abel to Zechariah *(Atonement)*

Glorification - Because they refused to rest under the wings of God's throne, Jesus, like Jeremiah, laments over the city from atop the mountain. He would come and desolate Jerusalem for her defiant violation of the Covenant, and tear down Herod's house *(Booths)*

COMMENTS

The patterns we have observed so far structure the life and ministry of Jesus Christ, but also the events of the first century. Jesus went through the pattern as head, and the firstfruits church followed Him as body. Together, their sacrifice founded a new Israel.

Notice that, just like the Ark, Jesus carried the sins of Israel into the wilderness and defeated their false god (Satan). Just like Israel in Babylon, Jesus died inside the "belly" of the empire.

But this "head" pattern was only the beginning of the firstfruits church.

JESUS AS HEAD OF
A NEW CREATION

Creation - Jesus is anointed by the Spirit at His baptism *(Sabbath)*

Division - As Moses, He is tested in the wilderness Himself, then prepares His people to make an exodus *(Passover)*

Ascension - Jesus transfigures the Law, builds a human Tabernacle, and establishes a new priesthood at the Last Supper *(Firstfruits)*

Testing - Jesus is crucified by the brief alliance of the Land beast (Priest/King) and Sea beast (Emperor). He dies under the condemnation of the Law of God *(Pentecost)*

Maturity - Jesus is resurrected. As Moses, He gathers His disciples and gives them a commission to conquer the Land *(Trumpets)*

Conquest - The Land of Israel is claimed for Christ. Herod dies on his throne *(Atonement)*

Glorification - The Apostles take the gospel to the Gentiles *(Booths)*

COMMENTS

Judgment begins at the house of God. What the church does "in secret" is rewarded openly by God, whether good or evil. In the Last Supper, we see Jesus prefiguring in the "Garden" of His new humanity the pattern of the Land, and later the World. Jesus exiles Judas as the second goat into the wilderness for destruction.

● **Creation** - The disciples follow a man carrying a jar of water to an upper room. Then they recline in the firmament, the Holy Place, with Jesus *(Sabbath)*

● **Division** - Jesus reveals that one of them is unclean and will betray Him. The disciples mourn *(Passover)*

● **Ascension** - Judas is singled out by Jesus, who gives him a warning (Law). Jesus breaks bread and tells them it is His body. He gives them wine and tells them it is His blood, poured out for the forgiveness of sins (Grace). His body and blood are divided, then reunited inside His people. As a holy warrior (Nazirite), He vows not to drink wine again until the fighting is over and He rests with His bride in the kingdom *(Firstfruits)*

● **Testing** - The disciples dispute about who will be the greatest in the kingdom. Jesus tells them they will be tested, but rule as kings *(Pentecost)*

● **Maturity** - They will now need swords and moneybags *(Trumpets)*

● **Conquest** - After the supper, Jesus washes their feet—in the Laver—to sanctify them as a new priesthood. Jesus hands Judas the dipped bread and Satan enters into him *(Atonement)*

● **Glorification** - They sing a hymn and go to the Mount of Olives, where Jesus predicts His death, the scattering of His followers, and His resurrection. As Bridegroom, He gives them a new commandment, to love each other as He loves them. He tells them that He is going to prepare a home for them *(Booths)*

COMMENTS

Jesus was arrested in a Garden. He was led before the Council and condemned by His own brothers (Land). He was then brought before Pilate, the Roman governor (World).

In John's gospel, when Pilate sits Jesus in the place of judgment, the Greek seems to be deliberately ambiguous as to who is the judge, Jesus or Pilate (John 19:13).

As with Abraham, Joseph and Daniel, the obedience of the suffering servant brought a nightmare to the Gentile ruler, or in this case, his wife. She warned Pilate to have nothing to do with "that just man."

Creation - The disciples sleep in darkness as Christ meets the serpent in the garden *(Sabbath)*

Division - Jesus is arrested at night. When He says, "I am He," to separate Himself, the soldiers fall to the ground as dead men. The disciples desert Him. The firstborn is taken *(Passover)*

Ascension - Jesus is taken to the house of the High Priest, mocked, beaten and condemned. When day comes, He is accused of claiming He would destroy the Temple and raise up a new one in three days *(Firstfruits)*

Testing - The Jews choose a "beast" for release instead of Jesus. He is crucified at the place of a skull. Here, the serpent's head is finally crushed under the foot of the offspring of the woman. The Law is satisfied *(Pentecost)*

Maturity - Jesus' nakedness covers the nakedness of Adam *(Trumpets)*

Conquest - Jesus is pierced with a spear, thrust through like a man or beast that dared approach the mountain of God (Exodus 19:12-13), so that we might approach freely as *men* (Hebrews 12:20-24). Again, the guarding soldiers are "dead men." As High Priest, Jesus leaves His Atonement linen on the angel-flanked lid of the "Ark" and puts on His robes of glory *(Atonement)*

Glorification - This cycle finishes where it began, in a garden. Mary mistakes Him for Adam, the gardener. Her life has come from His side as He slept. But she has met the Greater Solomon, the Bridegroom who unites heaven and earth *(Booths)*

THE CHURCH

WITH THE ASCENSION OF THE PROMISED SAVIOUR, human history moved into the next phase. There was now a Man at the right hand of the true Emperor, and He had been given all authority. The history of the Apostolic church was the fulfillment of Old Covenant Israel. From AD30 to AD70, a new army was mustered. As Day 5, this army was a summoning of faithful Jews (heavenly birds) and faithful Gentiles (fish plundered from the Sea).

Creation - A world united as one blood *(Sabbath)*

Division - A world divided by blood *(Passover)*

Ascension - A centralized priesthood *(Firstfruits)*

Testing - The harvest begins *(Pentecost)*

Maturity - A centralized priesthood *(Trumpets)*

The mark of the Old Covenant centralized priesthood was blood (death), because it was governed on earth. The blood pictured the Covenant *head*. The mark of the New Covenant centralized priesthood is water (resurrection), because it is governed from heaven. The water covers the whole Covenant *body*.

COMMENTS

The book of Acts, as a conquest of the empire-Land, contains many instances of the dominion pattern. Here is one of my favorites.

At the centre of the pattern, there is usually a ruler. Sometimes it is a beast in the wilderness. Here it is Jesus as the slain Lamb who conquered the beast in the wilderness.

The book of Acts consistently places baptism at **Atonement**, the Laver of the Tabernacle.

Creation - An angel commands Philip to go to Gaza at noon *(Sabbath)*

Division - Philip departs for a desert place. He miraculously runs to meet an Ethiopian eunuch's chariot *(Passover)*

Ascension - The eunuch is from his queen's court and in charge of treasure. He is returning from worship in Jerusalem. He invites Philip to come up and sit with him in his chariot *(Firstfruits)*

Testing - The eunuch is reading Isaiah's prophecy of the slain lamb of God *(Pentecost)*

Maturity - Philip explains the prophecy was about Jesus, and the eunuch is converted *(Trumpets)*

Conquest - The eunuch commands the chariot to stop, and Philip baptizes him. When they come up from the water, the Spirit takes Philip away *(Atonement)*

Glorification - The eunuch goes on his way rejoicing. Philip finds himself at Azotus and preaches the gospel in all the towns until he reaches Caesarea *(Booths)*

We are now at the point where we can understand the pattern of the church's foundation in the first century. AD30 to AD70 was a 40 year wilderness period for Israel in which the old body would be torn apart and a new body "incorporated."

The writer of Hebrews warns the Christian Jews not to look back to Herod's Egypt, or they would die in the wilderness like their ancestors.

The matrix means that the establishment and massacre of the early church recapitulates not only Israel's journey from slavery to Sabbath, but also the temptation in Eden. Those primeval "heads" had taken on bodies for one last-ditch rebellion. *Adam, Eve and the serpent* had grown to become institutions symbolized in the Revelation as *a false prophet, a prostitute and a beast.* Their bloody "Bronze Altar" kingdom was *De-Created* and replaced with a fragrant "Incense Altar" kingdom that would grow to fill the earth.

COMMENTS

In this pattern, you can also see a correspondence with 1 Samuel. At *Ascension*, the Ark's captivity finished off the old unfaithful priesthood of Eli, and its return at *Conquest* finished off the unfaithful kingdom of Saul.

Jesus judged Satan in the Garden at His crucifixion. His coming in judgment upon the Land occurred in AD70. His judgment upon the World is yet to come.

Creation - Ark: The birth, perfect life and ministry of the Word of God made flesh. Christ rules as **Moses** *(Sabbath)*

Division - Veil: Jesus dies on the cross for the sins of the world and is resurrected *(Passover)*

Ascension - He ascends to the right hand of the Father to rule Israel from the throne of **David**. Drawing near as High Priest, He receives the seven-sealed mystery of God *(Firstfruits)*

Testing - Lampstand: He opens the new Law, sending the Holy Spirit to indwell His people, filling them with light as His human Tabernacle, His body on earth. The new Israel is formed, tested and purified in a "wilderness" by Jewish persecution from without and Judaizing heresy from within *(Pentecost)*

Maturity - Incense: Both the Land and the Sea are plundered as Jews and Gentiles believe the gospel. An army of believers is mustered and martyred as holy warriors. Judgments begin to fall upon the Old Jerusalem and its empire-Tabernacle. Christ rules as **Joshua** *(Trumpets)*

Conquest - High Priest: The firstfruits church is resurrected, and their blood is avenged by God. Old Jerusalem is destroyed in a "flood" of Roman troops, (Daniel 9:26) and a New Jerusalem replaces her *(Atonement)*

Glorification - Shekinah: Christ now rules the world as **Solomon**. After a marriage supper in heaven, the ruling saints carry His sword-Word across the world *(Booths)*

Revelation employs the Bible Matrix at many levels, but here is its basic structure. Like Ezekiel, Revelation is about the death of old Israel and the reconquest of the Land by a resurrected Israel. In Ezekiel, the northern and southern tribes were "resurrected" as united "Jews." In the first century, it was Jews and Gentiles that were reunited in a new body.

When reading Revelation, it is best to substitute the word translated "earth" for Land. Up to chapter 19, the book is about the *De-Creation* of Herod's false worship in Israel. Chapters 20-21 concern the gospel age, during which Satan is bound from deceiving the nations any longer. This corresponds with the Lord giving the Canaanites into Joshua's hand. He was to take their Land as Israel's inheritance. The nations are Jesus' inheritance. If the world has not been conquered, it is because the church has not been entirely faithful. But history is far from over. The yeast will do its job.

COMMENTS

The placement of the letters to the churches puts the churches (as Lamps) as rulers in the new Holy Place.

The Revelation to John uses symbols from all previous Scripture—including the names and the numbers—to communicate the symbolic side of the first century history. A corrupted Jerusalem is again pictured as Jericho, but also as Babylon, and a priest's daughter who is to be burned with fire for her harlotry.

Like Ezekiel, Revelation ends with a vision of a Temple made of people. This time the "new Jerusalem" is the age of the church. The book begins with Greater Adam (Jesus) and ends with Greater Eve (the church).

Book of Revelation		First Century History
Vision of "Adam" *(A holy king)*	**Sabbath**	Ministry of Christ
Letters to churches *(Jesus passes over)*	**Passover**	Crucifixion/ Resurrection
Ascension *(The Lamb)*	**Firstfruits**	Ascension *(Law opened)*
7 Seals *(Gospel horses)*	**Pentecost**	Acts *(Law given)*
7 Trumpets *(Plagues/witnesses)*	**Trumpets**	*to* AD60's *(Law received)*
7 Bowls *(Harlot dethroned; Jesus & saints pass through)*	**Atonement**	AD70 *(Herods destroyed)*
Vision of "Eve" *(A holy nation)*	**Booths**	Church era begins

COMMENTS

This brings us to the completion of the whole-Bible pattern. The Old Covenant forms the house; the New Covenant fills the house. By the end of history, Jesus has redeemed the Garden, the Land and the World. At **Booths** (Tabernacles), the world will finally be a pure Temple for God. As the completed Tabernacle, it is shaped like a man, head and body, the whole Christ.

The destruction of Herod's Jericho by the firstfruits church was only the first conquest of the church. This has enormous implications for the interpretation of the "imminent" predictions of both Jesus and His Apostles in the New Testament. Based on this structure, and despite the unpopularity of this view, I believe that the first resurrection—of the Old Covenant saints and the martyred Apostles—occurred in AD70, replacing the angelic government who had administered the Law throughout the Old Testament. The elders before the throne are now resurrected human ones.

This current age is bookended by resurrections. The second resurrection and final judgment will occur at the end of history, when mankind will not only have been redeemed but brought to full maturity in Christ, able to govern perfectly under God.

So, beginning with the resurrection of Jesus, we have resurrection in Garden, Land (AD70) and, finally, World.

Between the Land and World judgments, church history is one very long Day of Atonement, with the complete High Priest, head and body, standing in the open veil with His foot on the beast's neck. The strong man is bound from deceiving the nations, and Christ's gospel is spoiling his goods. Symbolically, the sun is standing still until the victory of Joshua is complete.

ARK
Creation - World united as one blood   *(Sabbath)*
NOAH

VEIL
Division - World divided by blood   *(Passover)*
ABRAHAM - CIRCUMCISION - HEAD

BRONZE ALTAR
Ascension - Centralized priesthood *(Firstfruits)*
ISRAEL - EARTHLY MEDIATORS

LAMPSTAND
Testing - The harvest begins   *(Pentecost)*
THE CHRIST

INCENSE ALTAR
Maturity - Centralized priesthood   *(Trumpets)*
FIRSTFRUITS CHURCH -
HEAVENLY MEDIATORS

LAVER
Conquest - World divided by water *(Atonement)*
THE WHOLE CHRIST - BAPTISM - BODY

REST
Glorification - World united by one Spirit *(Booths)*
ETERNITY

The
Whole
Christ

The weekly, corporate, New Covenant worship of the church is based upon Israel's Old Covenant worship. In our worship, we recapitulate the Creation Week. Our obedience in the Garden transforms the Land and the World.

A PATTERN FOR WORSHIP

Creation - The saints are officially called to worship *(Sabbath)*

  Division - Corporate confession and forgiveness *(Passover)*

    Ascension - By faith, the saints ascend before the throne in heaven, singing praises *(Firstfruits)*

      Testing - The Word is taught *(Pentecost)*

      Maturity - The offering is taken *(Trumpets)*

    Conquest - Communion is celebrated *(Atonement)*

  Glorification - Thanksgiving prayer and a recommission to preach the gospel *(Booths)*

BLUEPRINT FOR VICTORY

A CHRISTIAN FUTURE

A CLOSE FRIEND SAID I WAS LIKE THE MAIN CHARACTER in the movie *A Beautiful Mind*, desperately looking for patterns of conspiracy in the newspaper clippings pinned all over the walls of his shed. Well, the Bible's patterns appear far too frequently to be imaginary or coincidental. And, once they are identified, even the obscure chapters and weird visions suddenly carry great relevance for today.

These undeniable patterns enable us to interpret the Bible correctly, and this approach leads inexorably to the conclusion that Christ reigns now, and that there will be a gradual, visible victory for His church.

Jesus Christ rules the world, but most Christians act like His kingdom is yet to come. They are expecting this gospel age to end in defeat. However, as you have hopefully observed, the Bible's own historical and literary patterns lead us to expect victory in this age, *in history*, before Christ returns.

Even though Christians agree on the fundamentals, there are conflicting approaches to interpreting "the big picture." So who is right and does it matter? Shouldn't we forget about trying to work it out and get on with the job?

The problem is, getting the big picture wrong makes it harder to get on with the job. If we expect historical defeat, we'll get it. It also robs us of the things God has given us to spur us on. It subtly abandons the very earthy, *physical* commission of Christ and settles for a faith that is fundamentally disconnected from **reality**. The Lord's mandate to both Adam and the Apostles was domination of the *physical world.*

Western culture is dying not because the end of the world is near, but because the western church has swapped her physical inheritance for a Christianity that is, well, *somewhere else.* For many, Christianity is in the head, in the heart, or in heaven—anywhere but *here* on earth. Misunderstanding the fearless, strategic **takeover-by-sacrifice** that Christ commanded leaves many Christians without the vision, tools or confidence to build and maintain a long term cultural legacy. Yet these are our *heritage.*

Rediscovering our **identity** is the solution for our lack of confidence. Israel's history is most assuredly our history, as much as a narrow trunk suddenly fills the sky with branches. This theme of trunk and branches, Adam and Eve, head and body, Old Testament and New, Christ and the church—the *Whole Christ*—is also found in the deep structure (based on Genesis 1) that undergirds the entire Bible, and the New Testament is but the final, majestic sweep. To regain her identity, the church must develop not only an intimate knowledge of the Old Testament, but one that is *totally* integrated with the New. Peter Leithart writes:

"Recovering the Old Testament as a text in which Christians live and move and have their being is one of the most urgent tasks before the church. Reading the Reformers is good and right. Christian political activism has its place. Even at their best, however, these can only bruise the heel of a world that has abandoned God. But the Bible—the Bible is a sword to divide joints from marrow, a weapon to crush the head."[1]

The modern church ignores most of the Bible, with the result that the teachings and culture of the world flood in to fill the void. Only as Christians think, eat, live and breathe the Scriptures will we again see a godly culture begin to form around the church.

I hope this little book helps to give modern Christians a big handle on the Bible, and the faith to construct a world based upon the heavenly pattern seen by John on the mountain. By the power of the Spirit, the Great Commission will succeed.

---

1 Peter J. Leithart, *The Kingdom and the Power,* p. 93.

27

RECOMMENDED READING AND LISTENING

James B. Jordan

Through New Eyes: Developing A Biblical View Of The World

Creation In Six Days: A Defense Of The Traditional Reading Of Genesis One

Primeval Saints: Studies In The Patriarchs of Genesis

Judges: A Practical And Theological Commentary

The Handwriting On The Wall: A Commentary On The Book Of Daniel

The Vindication of Jesus Christ: A Brief Reader's Guide To Revelation

Biblical Horizons lectures at www.wordmp3.com

Peter J. Leithart

A House For My Name: A Survey Of The Old Testament

Blessed Are The Hungry: Meditations On The Lord's Supper

A Son To Me: An Exposition of 1 & 2 Samuel

1 & 2 Kings: Brazos Theological Commentary On The Bible

The Promise Of His Appearing: An Exposition Of Second Peter

The Kingdom And The Power: Rediscovering The Centrality Of The Church

Kenneth L. Gentry, Jr.

Before Jerusalem Fell: Dating The Book Of Revelation

He Shall Have Dominion: A Postmillennial Eschatology

Gary DeMar

Last Days Madness: Obsession Of The Modern Church

David Chilton

Paradise Restored: A Biblical Theology Of Dominion

The Days Of Vengeance: An Exposition Of The Book Of Revelation

David A. Dorsey

The Literary Structure Of The Old Testament

Michael Bull

Totus Christus: A Biblical Theology of the Whole Christ

CPSIA information can be obtained at www.ICGtesting.com
Printed in the USA
LVOW12s2206150914

404228LV00001B/105/P